RESEARCH AND TECHNICAL LIBRARIES
Organisation, Operation and Services

RESEARCH AND TECHNICAL LIBRARIES

Organisation, Operation and Services

Meghna Dhar

Lecturer,

P.G. Department of Library & Information Science,

University of Jammu

J & K State.

Ess Ess Publications

New Delhi

Research and Technical Libraries
Organisation, Operation and Services

ISBN: 978-81-7000-604-6

Rs.675/-

First Published 2010

Published by:
Ess Ess Publications
4837/24, Ansari Road,
Darya Ganj,
New Delhi-110 002.
INDIA
Phones: 23260807, 41563444
Fax: 41563334
E-mail: info@essessreference.com
www.essessreference.com

Cover Design by Patch Creative Unit

Printed and bound in India at Salasar Imaging Systems.

"A Good Book Requires
One Good Eye,
One Good Light Source,
and
One Good Finger."

Contents

PREFACE

Libraries the "Power House" of generating information are regarded as the heart of any institute. Libraries are not merely storehouse of reading material collected for preservation but it functions as a dynamic instrument of education to feed the intellect of the students, encourage the researchers of the faculty and invite all who enter its house to partake fully of its intellectual and cultural contents. These are regarded as the backbone of any research organization and it helps in the advancement of R&D activities in which information is the most important aspect. Research and technical libraries are universally recognized as repository of knowledge and an integral part of education, society and research. The frontiers of knowledge are ever increasing and to meet the information needs of the scientists and researchers comprehensively, the librarians are required to acquire suitable and sufficient quantity of collection in their areas of interest.

The author has the privilege of teaching experience of the subject R&T libraries and this work is an outcome of that experience. One hopes that all this effort might prove helpful to the student community and the librarians. The teachers of library and information science will also find this work equally useful. Efforts have been made to cover all the important topics. The text incorporates fifteen chapters starting with the First chapter as an introduction which includes various types of libraries, difference between a special and a general library; types, functions and services of special libraries.

Chapter 2nd deals with definitions, kinds, characteristics, objectives, organizational pattern and functions of R&T libraries. Chapter 3rd describes the history and development of Research and Technical libraries. Chapter 4th is concerned with place of Research and technical libraries in knowledge society. Chapter 5 describes the concept of Resource Sharing and Networking –its need, basic requirements and usefulness in R&T libraries.

Two chapters that is 6th and 7th, on automation has been included to enable the students to have a glimpse at the impact of Information Technology in all the spheres of R&T library operations and services. It also deals with the role of INTERNET in the present scenario.

In the "Organization and Administration" part of the book detailed activities, routines and operations of different sections of R&T libraries have been described along with specimen for routine operations to enable library workers to streamline and uniformise their operations and services. Chapter 9th is concerned with Planning and acquisition of R&T libraries equipment. Chapter 10th deals with Personnel Management and Chapter 11th describes the finance and budget in R&T libraries.

Chapter 12th, 13th, 14th and 15th deals with Organization and Working of Acquisition section, Technical Section, Periodical section and Reference section in R&T libraries.

This book is written primarily for the Post-graduate students of Library and Information Science and an attempt is made to cover almost all the aspects of R&T libraries as per the syllabi of M.L.ISc degree of the Indian Universities.

In the end, I request all my friends and readers to kindly send their constructive suggestions in case any deficiency is observed, this would add to the author's sense of humility as a learner and ensure necessary rectification in future.

Hope this book turns out to be a "good book which is opened with expectations and closed with profit."

- Meghna Dhar

ACKNOWLEDGEMENTS

The present work is a product of inspiration, encouragement and assistance from various sources. I owe my deep sense of gratitude to my father Dr. M.L. Dhar, my mother Mrs. Sheela Dhar and my dear sister Ms. Ruby Dhar for providing me conducive atmosphere, constant encouragement and inspiration to complete this work. I express my sincerest gratitude to my teachers, Prof. I.V. Malhan and Prof. Sangeeta Gupta, Department of Library and Information Science University of Jammu, Jammu for giving me an opportunity to teach this subject in the Department, which has resulted in the outcome of this book.

It gives me immense pleasure to acknowledge my colleague Dr. Shivarama Roa K. who has been generous enough in providing supporting facts, suggestions and whose inspiring personality have influenced me and my work. The author acknowledge her deep debt of gratitude to various eminent authors whose standard works have been consulted and quoted in this book.

I wish to acknowledge the services of Miss Neeru Singh for carefully composing the manuscript.

Finally, my thanks are also due to M/s Ess Ess Publications, New Delhi, for publishing and bringing out this book so neatly and expeditiously in the best format within a short span of time.

- Meghna Dhar

List of Abbreviation and Acronyms Used

ADI	-	American Documentation Institute.
ADINET	-	Ahmedabad Library Network.
ALA	-	American Library Association.
ARPANET	-	Advanced Research Project Networks.
ASLIB	-	Association for Information Management.
ASIS	-	American Society for Information Science.
BARC	-	Bhabha Atomic Research Centre.
BBS	-	Bulletin Board Service.
BC	-	Bibliographic Classification.
BHEL	-	Bharat Heavy Electricals Ltd.
BNB	-	British National Bibliography.
BONET	-	Bombay Library Network.
CALIBNET	-	Calcutta Library Network.
CAS	-	Current Awareness Service.
CC	-	Colon Classification.
CCF	-	Common Communication Format.
CD-ROM	-	Compact Disk Read Only Memory.
CFTRI	-	Central Food Technology Research Institute

CSIR	-	Council of Scientific and Industrial Research.
DDC	-	Dewey Decimal Classification.
DELNET	-	Developing Library Network.
DESIDOC	-	Defence Science Information Documentation Centre.
DOE	-	Department of Electronic
DRDO	-	Defence Research and Developing Organisation.
DVD	-	Digital Versatile Disk (Formerly Digital Video Disk)
E-Journal	-	Electronic Journal.
E-mail	-	Electronic Mailing.
E-publishing	-	Electronic Publishing
ERNET	-	Education & Research Network.
FTP	-	File Transfer Protocol.
GSI	-	Geological Survey of India.
HMT	-	Hindustan Machine Tools.
HTML	-	Hypertext Mark-up Language.
IARI	-	Indian Veterinary Research Institute.
ICAR	-	Indian Council of Agricultural Research.
ICHR	-	Indian Council of Historical Research.
ICMR	-	Indian Council of Medical Research.
ICSSR	-	Indian Council of Social Sciences Research.
ILL	-	Inter Library Loan.
IISc	-	Indian Institute of Science.
INB	-	Indian National Bibliography.
INFLIBNET	-	Information Library Network.

INSDOC	-	Indian National Scientific Documentation Centre.
IIT's	-	Indian Institute of Technology.
IASLIC	-	Indian Association of Special Library and Information Centre.
ISALIC	-	Indian Association of Special Library and Information Centre.
IT	-	Information Technology.
LA	-	Library Association.
LAN	-	Local Area Network.
LC	-	Library of Congress.
MALIBNET	-	Madras Library Network.
MAN	-	Metropolitan Area Network.
MARC	-	Machine Readable Catalogue
MCLC	-	Mysore City Library Consortium
NASSDOC	-	National Social Science Documentation Centre.
NICNET	-	National Information Centre Network.
NISCAIR	-	National Institute of Science Communication and Information Resources.
NISSAT	-	National Information System for Science and Technology.
NSF	-	National Science Foundation.
OCLC	-	Online Public Access Catalogue.
R&D	-	Research and Development.
RIFD	-	Radio Frequency Identification.
R& T	-	Research and Technical.
SC	-	Subject Classification.

SDI	-	Selective Dissemination of Information.
SENDOC	-	Small Enterprises National Documentation Centre.
SIRNET	-	Scientific and Industrial Research Network.
SLA	-	Special Library Association.
SSDC	-	Social Science Documentation Centre.
TCP/IP	-	Transmission on Control Protocol/ Internet Protocol.
UGC- INFONET	-	University Grants Commission-Information Network.
UNESCO	-	United Nations Educational, Scientific and Cultural Organisation.
WAN	-	Wide Area Network.
WWW	-	World Wide Web.
WHO	-	World Health Organization.

1

INTRODUCTION

Libraries the 'Power House' of generating information are regarded as the heart of any institute. Libraries are not merely store-house of reading material collected for preservation but it functions as a dynamic instrument of education to feed the intellect of the student, encourage the researchers of the faculty and invite all who enter its house to partake fully of its intellectual and cultural contents. These are universally recognized as an important social institutions. No community is considered complete without a library. The gradual spread of education, the intensification of research activities and rapid increase in production of recorded knowledge have led to the expansion of libraries and the development of their services. Today, libraries play a significant role in the socio-economic, scientific and technological development of a country.

1.1 TYPES OF LIBRARIES

A library is a collection of information, sources, resources and services, and the structure in which it is housed : it is organized for use and maintained by a public body, an institution, or a private individual. In the more traditional sense, a library is a collection of books. The term collection may be, the building that houses such a collection or both. The library system of a country covers the different types of libraries that come into existence in response of social needs. Modern libraries are organized and maintained for catering to the requirements of different communities -the general public, academicians and students, research workers, businessmen, specialists and others. The major types of libraries that are normally found in a library system of a country can be enumerated as Public, Academic, Special and National libraries. The graphic representation of various types of libraries is shown in Fig 1.1

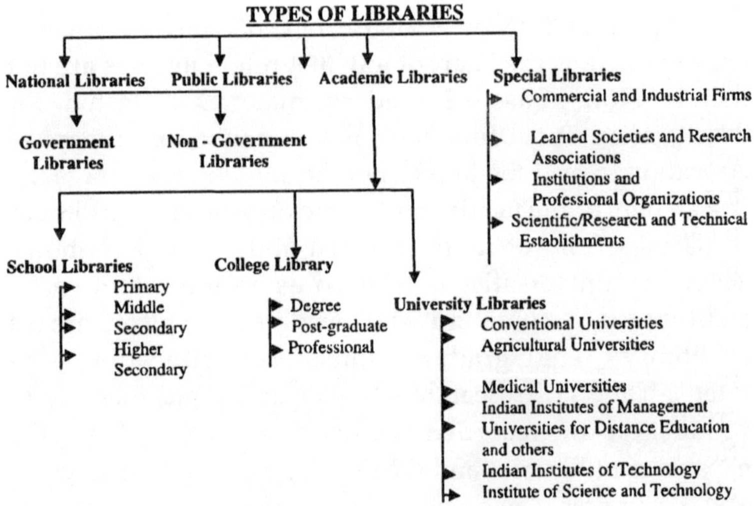

Fig. 1.1. Types of Libraries

1.1.1 National Libraries

The National library of a country is distinct from other types of libraries. It is financed and maintained out of government funds of a country and exists to serve the whole nation. The books in such libraries are meant for reference purpose only and are usually copyright libraries. The national library is normally very large one having millions of books and other materials. A national library is therefore the biggest and best power-house for generating knowledge for the nation. Its main function is to acquire and preserve everything concerning the country whether they are published or produced locally or abroad and also serves as a permanent depository for the countries outstanding and most complete collection of the national libraries. Some of the examples of national libraries are The Library of Congress (LC), Washington D.C, The British Library of United Kingdom, The National Library of India, Kolkata etc.

1.1.2 Public Libraries

Public library is a People's University for those who laid stress on educative aspect, it is a common man's cultural centre for those who had in mind its recreational role, for some it is a centre to provide authentic information for various aspects of life. Thus, a public library simply means 'a library meant for public use'. It is a living force for education, culture and information. It is a life long learning institute. Public libraries cover all fields of knowledge which are meant for public use. It is a library for all irrespective of age, profession, race, sex, colour or creed, nationality, language or social status. The main functions of a public library is to serve as a centre for information, self-education, culture, local cultural materials, development of understanding democratic spirit and being an impartial service agency.

1.1.3 Academic Libraries

Academic libraries are libraries of school, college and similar educational institutions which are primarily intended for the dissemination of information and knowledge. The school libraries serve many ends that is enrichment of teaching by provision of illustrative background material suitable for class-room use and display, instruction and practice in the use of books and of a library, development of pupils personal interest's, creating of reading habits in the children etc. The college libraries are generally intended for the use of academic staffs and undergraduates. The primary function of the college library is to help the college in carrying out its programme. The university library forms the apex of academic libraries. A university is the highest institution for teaching and research and makes direct contribution to the advancement of knowledge. It is a scholastic library and good library is therefore a necessity because it plays a significant role in dissemination and conservation of information and knowledge.

1.1.4 Special Libraries

Special libraries and information centers are a natural outcome of the need for information support to research and development, business and industry, expanded functions of governments and similar other organizations. Special libraries are primarily intended for limited clientele with special field of interest. The term special libraries denotes specialist libraries. A special library is the one which is specializing in a particular subject or group of subjects or a particular form of documents. These Libraries are also restricted to specific professional or academic group of users whose information needs are defined by a particular subject or activity. Special libraries are formed in research and development establishments, government departments, directorates, industrial and business undertakings, learned societies and professional associations, trade and business associations, hospitals and health services, social and welfare organizations, museums, national gallery of arts etc.

L.M. Harrod in his "Librarian's Glossary of Terms" defined that a "Special Library is a collection of books and other printed, graphic or recorded material dealing with a limited field of knowledge and provided by a learned society research organisation, industrial or commercial undertaking, government department or even and educational institution. It may also be a special branch of a public library serving certain interests or occupational groups such as a technical library or a special subject library, meeting the needs of all enquiries on that given subject such as a music library".

D.J. Foskett defines a special library as "one serving a group, having an extra-library, existence, whose members direct at least some of their activities towards a common purpose. This excludes academic libraries as their users pursue their individual ends and are in no sense united by a common purpose."

Broadfield defines special library as a "library that is neither academic, commercial national or public but it intends to serve the needs of a portion of a community requiring detailed information on a limited subject field.".

According to **Reitz's, Dictionary of Library and Information Science, 2005**, a "Special Library is established and funded by a commercial firm, private association, government agency, non-print organization or special interest group to meet the information needs of its employees members or staff in accordance with the organizations missions and goals."

1.2 DIFFERENCE BETWEEN A SPECIAL AND A GENERAL LIBRARY

A special Library files information contained in documents. On the other hand, a general library is concerned with documents. In case of special libraries information requires the application of special techniques for storage, retrieval and dissemination. Special libraries are generally concerned with micro-documents such as periodicals, reports, standards etc A general library is concerned with both micro and marco-documents. In case of special libraries users information requirements are specific where as in case of general libraries information requirements of users are general. One major difference is that the special libraries offers services only to the staff of their parent organisation and in case of general library a widely distributed group of users are served.

1.3 TYPES OF SPECIAL LIBRARIES

We may recognize the following types of Special Libraries :-

1. Libraries of Commercial and Industrial firms.
2. Libraries Learned Societies and Research Association.
3. Libraries of Institutions and Professional Organziation.
4. Libraries of Government agencies and departments.
5. Libraries of Scientific/ Research and Technical establishments.

The types of special libraries are too numerous to mention. In short, we may say that the special libraries are located in business, industrial and scientific research and industrial manufacture, law firms, medical and health institutions, press, museums, agriculture sector, international organizations, advocacy organisations, large corporations, professional associations, research centres, defence sector, national gallery of arts, social and welfare orgranisations etc.

There are many libraries in India attached to various commercial, industrial, scientific, technical and research organizations, Libraries attached to the Tata- Iron and Steel Company, Jamshedpur, Hindustan Steel ltd, Bangalore, Indian Institute of Science, Bangalore, Indian Institute of Packaging, Mumbai, Bhaba Atomic Research Institute Mumbai, Bhaba Atomic Research Institute Mumbai,

National Physical Laboratory, Delhi; Geological Survey of India, Kolkata; DESIDOC Delhi, NISCAIR Delhi etc. are some typical examples.

1.4 FUNCTIONS OF SPECIAL LIBRARIES

The special libraries have to perform the following functions:-

1. To supply their specific group of readers with up-to-date specialized pieces of information in the field of knowledge served by the library;
2. To analyse, synthesize and evaluate information and data;
3. To provide critical reviews, monographs, reports and/or collections;
4. To provide critical compilations;
5. To provide replies to queries;
6. To provide reprints, bibliographies and references;
7. To help research workers in the works of translation, abstraction, documentation, photographic reproduction;
8. Provision of CAS and SDI Services;
9. To procure literature on the latest developments, all over the world by way of purchase, gift and co-operation with the counter parts of other countries and make these available to their own readers;
10. To arrange specialized books and other material on inter-library loan system.

1.5 COLLECTION OF SPECIAL LIBRARIES

The collection of special libraries deals with the books and other printed, graphic or recorded material dealing with limited field knowledge. The collection deals with special kinds of documents such as Braille books, audio-visual material, maps, books published in many languages, periodicals, journals, standards, technical reports, monographs, patents, newspaper clippings, manuscripts, reference material etc. The micro-documents are given much preference as compared to macro-documents.

1.6 SERVICES OF SPECIAL LIBRARIES

Various services which are offered by special libraries may be stated as under:-

General Services i.e. Acquisition, technical processing and circulation, Referral and Reference service, CAS, SDI, Reprography, Abstracting, and Indexing Service, Routing of Periodicals, Reproduction of table of contents, Book reviews, Translation Service, Literature Search, Newspaper Clipping Service, Inter-library loan service etc.

Thus, the major and perhaps the only objective of special library is the provision of information in support of the objectives of its parent organisation. Although special libraries exist in a wide variety of organizations, most of them being units of larger organizations but these are established to serve only a particular group of users or specialists working on a subject or a group of subjects or on a particular type of documents.

2

Research And Technical Libraries - Its Concept

2.1 INTRODUCTION

Library is the backbone of any research organization and it helps in the advancement of R&D activities in which information is the most important aspect. Research and technical libraries are recognized as repository of knowledge and an integral part of education, society and research. The frontiers of knowledge are ever increasing. It is more so in various branches of science and technology, social-sciences and humanities in which researchers are going on throughout the world in quest of new knowledge. All the researchers and technologists require latest and relevant information to keep themselves abreast of new developments in their respective areas of interest. To meet the information needs of the scientists and researchers comprehensively, the libraries are required to acquire suitable and sufficient quantity of collection in their areas of interest.

2.2 DEFINITIONS

According to Harrod's Librarians Glossary, 1990,

Technical library is a library containing mostly books of a technical nature. When connected with a public library, it may be a section of the reference library or separate department in the central building or a separate building. The library generally consists of a specialized documents and provides facilities for undertaking exhaustive investigation. It may also provide referral services in support of studies in subject fields connected with developments, tests, engineering and evaluation as well as research.

Reitz's Dictionary of Library and Information Science,2005, states that "Technical library is a library that supports one or more of the applied science, such as engineering or computer science. A technical library can be a branch in a large university, a major collection within a large academic or public library or a special library or a special library maintained by a private corporation or government agency"

According to **Title II, Part C of the Higher Education Act,** " a research library is a library that supports one or more of the applied sciences, such as engineering or computer science. A technical library can be a branch in a large university, a major collection within a large academic or public library or a special library maintained by a private corporation or government agency"

2.3 KINDS OF RESEARCH AND TECHNICAL LIBRARIES

Different kinds of Research and Technical libraries attached to various Research and Technical Institutions are as under:-

- **Libraries of Research Councils**
  - Indian Council of Agricultural Research (ICAR). Delhi.

- Council of Scientific and Industrial Research Headquarters, New Delhi (CSIR)
- Indian Council of Social Sciences Research (ICSSR), Delhi.
- Indian Council of Historical Research (ICHR), Delhi
- Indian Council of Medical Research (ICMR), Delhi.

• **Learned Societies, Research Organizations and Documentation Centre's Libraries**
  - Central Scientific Instruments Organization, Chandigarh.
  - Defence Scientific Information and Documentation Centre.
  - National Science Library of NISCAIR.
  - The Library of World Health Organization.
  - Engineering Society, New York City.
  - The Library of the Royal Society of Medicine, London.
  - National Social Science Documentation Centre , New Delhi.
  - The Library of Royal Society Medicine, London.
  - National Science Foundation, USA.
  - Special Library Association, USA.
  - American Society of Information Science, USA.
  - Association of Information Management, U.K.

• **Libraries in the Areas of Agriculture Sector**
  - Andhra-Pradesh Agricultural University, Hyderabad.
  - G.B. Pant University of Agriculture and Technology Library Pant Nagar.

- Indian Agriculture Research Institute, Pusa, Delhi.
- Haryana Agriculture University, Hissar.
- Punjab Agricultural University, Ludhiana.
- Indira-Gandhi Krishi Vishwa Vidyalay, Madhya-Pradesh.
- Sher-i-Kashmir Agricultural University, J&K.

• **Libraries of Research Institutes and Research Laboratories**

- Bhabha Atomic Research Centre, Mumbai.
- Central Building Research Institute, Roorkee.
- Central Drug Research Institute, Lucknow.
- Central Food Technologies Research Institute, Mysore.
- Central Leather Research Institute, Chennai.
- Central Machine Tools Institute, Bangalore.
- Central Road Research Institute, Delhi.
- Central Aero-space Research Institute, Bangalore.
- Central Potato Research Institute, Shimla, H.P.
- Indian Institute of Technology, Mumbai.
- Indian Institute of Technology, New Delhi.
- Indian Standards Institute, New Delhi.
- Indian Veterniary Research Institute, Izatnagar, U.P.
- National Institute of Oceanography, Goa.
- Birla Institute of Technology, Ranchi, Bihar.
- Regional Research Laboratory, Jammu, J&K.
- Regional Research Laboratory, Hyderabad.
- National Aeronautical Laboratory, Delhi.
- National Chemical Laboratory, Poona.

  - National Physical Laboratory, Delhi.
  - National Research Laboratory, Washington, D.C.
  - Defence Electronics Research Laboratory, Bangalore.
  - Indian Institute of Science, Bangalore.
  - National Metallurigical Laboratory, Jamshedpur
- **Libraries of Industrial and Commercial Firms**
  - Bharat Heavy Electricals Ltd. Hardiwar.
  - Tata Institute of Fundamental Research, Mumbai.
  - Hindustan Aeronautics Ltd. , Bangalore.
  - Steel Authority of India, Ltd.
  - Hindustan Machine Tools, Bangalore.
- **Libraries of Other Scientific and Technical Establishments**
  - National Medical Library, New Delhi.
  - Geological Survey of India, Kolkatta.
  - National Library of Medicine, America.
  - US Geological Survey, U.S.
  - The Science Library Wing of the National in Kolkatta.

Thus, research and technical libraries are divided into two kinds that is those which are independent in themselves and those which are part of or related to general public or university libraries. They can also be classified into three groups that is professional, industrial and government.

2.4 CHARACTERISTICS OF RESEARCH AND TECHNICAL LIBRARIES

In a broad sense, research and technical libraries are frequently considered as special libraries, even though they are part of general academic and research institutions. This is primarily because scientific and technical libraries deal with information sources in specific subject areas and because they serve a restricted users with a rather narrow range of interests and with specific needs for particular pieces of information.

Following are different characteristics of research and technical libraries:

(i) Location

R&T libraries are located in business, industrial and scientific organizations dealing with scientific research and industrial manufacture as well as government departments, professional associations, learned societies and institutions.

(ii) Collection

The collection in R&T libraries is concerned with the single definite subject field. Though collection is limited but it is concerned with specialized collection of documents. The collection is mostly primary sources of information such as periodicals, journals, research monographs, technical reports, dissertations, theses, patents, conference papers documentation lists etc, and are considered to be most important for scientists. In case of R&T libraries general books and text-books are not encouraged as teaching is not the objective of the institution with which R&T libraries are concerned. However high quality of monographs and general books are recommended in these libraries. Besides research journals R&T libraries are supposed to compile its own tools and directories and also undertake documentation activities.

(iii) Users

The users of the R&T libraries are limited in number. They are normally the full-time employees of the institutions with which the library is concerned. The users are specialists in nature and their information requirements are specific. The users are generally engaged in fulfilling the aims and objectives of the institution in which they are working. Their information requirements may change from time to time depending upon the project work assigned to them by the institution.

(iv) Staff

The staff of R&T libraries should possess subject knowledge, especially of technical terms concerning with the field of specialization of the parent body. He/She must know the information requirements of the users. They must have proficiency in more than two languages and should possess skill in library techniques with special reference to indexing, abstracting, writing of reports, carrying out literature surveys and literature searches.

2.5 OBJECTIVES OF R&T LIBRARIES

R&T libraries are integral part of research. It is considered as the backbone of research. For research work free flow of information is required and this is possible only through various kinds of information services such as abstracting and indexing of journals, CAS, SDI, bibliographic and documentation services, resources sharing, reprographic services, referral services and translation services.

Following are the main objectives of R&T libraries.

(i) To acquire bibliographic materials related to the interests of specific kind of users.

(ii) To organize and display all the bibliographic materials in various ways and to make them available to users.

According to **Hamburg** and his **associates,** R&T libraries should take dynamic role in achieving the following objectives:

(i) To maximize accessibility of materials to users.

(ii) To maximize exposure of users to materials.

2.6 ORGANIZATIONAL PATTERN OF R&T LIBRARIES

The organizational pattern of a research and technical libraries is as under:

The Chief Executive under whom the whole organization of Research & Technical library functions is under the administrative control of Research Advisory Council and Management Council. The other relations with Advisory Committee are Director, Library Committee. The administration of R&T libraries is responsible for overall activities of the library such as planning, organizing, staffing, directing, co-ordinating, reporting and budgeting. The functional organizational structure of R&T libraries has been divided into following categories:-

(i) Technical Services.

(ii) Routine Processing.

(iii) Documentation and Information Services.

(i) Technical services comprises the functions of selection, acquisition, classification, cataloguing, and indexing.

The acquisition function consists of activities related to the selection of library materials and of all that is involved in the acquisition by purchase, gift, exchange or deposit. Cataloguing and classification are the functions associated with the identification and description of the library materials and their organization through classification.

(ii) Routine Processing is associated with preparation of books for shelving, catalogue card filing, maintenance and binding. Binding is concerned with the broader function of care and preservation of library collections.

(iii) Documentation and Information Services comprises of various functions such as circulation, document supply, reference and bibliography, newspaper clipping service, CAS, SDI, indexing and abstracting services, translation service, computer based information services, reprographic service, users education programmes, preparation of current content lists and documentation lists and routing of periodicals.

The graphic representation of organizational and functional chart of a Research and Technical library attached to a research organization is given in Fig 2.1.

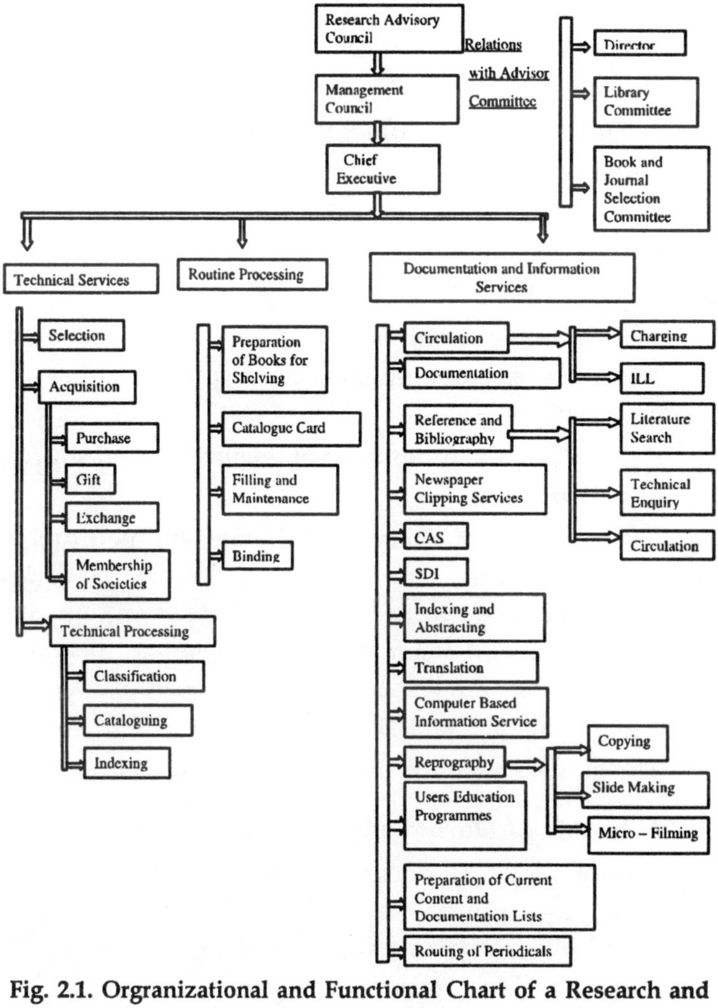

Fig. 2.1. Orgranizational and Functional Chart of a Research and Technical Library Attached to a Research Organization.

2.7 FUNCTIONS OF RESEARCH AND TECHNICAL LIBRARIES

Research and Technical libraries is an active organization which performs all kinds of functions to facilitate easy, convenient and comprehensive access to information so that research requirements of their users are fulfilled. In order to fulfill various objectives, research and technical library has to perform following functions:-

(i) Selection of documents and sources of data/ information,

(ii) Acquisition of documents and sources of data/ information,

(iii) Technical Processing of documents and sources of data/information,

(iv) Organization and storage of documents data and sources of information,

(v) Retrieval of documents data and sources of information,

(vi) Publication of reproduction of documents and sources of information.

The above term documents denote the medium by means of which data, information and knowledge are recorded. Data refers to raw facts and observations, and when data is intellectually processed it becomes information. The longest-lived and persistent kind of information becomes knowledge.

The above functions may be explained as under:-

(i) Selection of Documents

To select relevant documents and scan every possible source ranging from books, reference books, periodicals, reports and other publications in order to develop a good collection.

(ii) Acquisition of Documents

To acquire documents or literature on the latest developments all over the world by the way of purchase, gift, exchange, membership of socities and other organizations. The material acquired by the library is highly specialized pieces of information contained in periodicals, government and technical reports, newspaper cuttings, illustrations, conference papers and even unpublished materials for specific needs of users.

(iii) Technical Processing of Documents

To classify, catalogue and index all the documents acquired by the library.

(iv) Organisation and Storage of Documents

To organize and store all the documents after being classified and catalogued. That is to be placed on proper shelf or file in a drawer or a box.

(v) Retrieval of Documents

To supply specific group of readers with up-to-date specialized pieces of information in the field of knowledge served by the library.

(vi) Publication of Reproduction of Documents

To disseminate information, publications are reproduced by taking information from the documents retrieved by the readers.

Besides the above functions the research and technical libraries performs the following other functions:-

(i) To help research workers in the works of translations for highly specialized literature useful to the institutions especially for translation of foreign language publications.

(ii) Circulation of documents and routing of periodicals

for dissemination of information.

(iii) To compile exhaustive bibliographies pertaining to the fields of knowledge served by library.

(iv) To undertake large scale documentation of current literature (i.e. CAS) relevant to the institution. This involves compilation of Current Content Lists/ Documentation lists. The list may be typed, cyclostyled or printed.

(v) To regularly scan the literature searching tools such as bibliographies, indexing and abstracting periodicals and to prepare the files useful for the organisation.

(vi) To procure documents from the other institutions on ILL basis or exchange basis for the benefit of the users if the material is not available in the parent library.

(vii) To assist the researchers in making the contacts with the other specialists at national and international level.

(viii) Maintenance of reference and referral service and maintenance of special subject references, files and indexes.

(ix) To keep its users in touch with the similar projects going on at National and International level.

(x) Dissemination of currently published information by means of personal notifications, preparation and distribution of library bulletins and provision of special service publications.

(xi) To provide Selective Dissemination of Information (SDI) Service.

(xii) To assist users in making use of library material by providing users education programmes.

(xiii) To provide reprographical service that is reproduction of reading material needed by users.

CONCLUSION

Thus, Research and Technical libraries is expected to procure, process, store, retrieve and disseminate information, documents and data. It aims at providing required information pin pointedly, exhaustively and promptly in a useable form. For this purpose the library has to build up its collection in order to meet the users requirements.

3

History and Development of Research and Technical Libraries

3.1 EARLY DEVELOPMENTS

The history of libraries parallels the history of writing. For over 5,000 years human beings have made pictorial or written records of their ideas, their environments and their discoveries, on various types of materials such as clay, metal, wood papyrus, bone, silk, parchment, leather, paper etc. During all stages of development, these records have been collected in various libraries.

As to the earliest recorded scientific and technical writings, they are also in the form of inscriptions on clay tablets, papyrus and parchment. Many cuneiform tablets of Babylonian origin have been discovered which deal with mathematics, some of these dating to 1800-1600 B.C. The Chinese developed a sophisticated civilization for back in ancient times, a full documentary study of all branches of science, technology, chemistry, biology, agriculture and medicine. Early Egyption papyrus reveal a scientific interest in subjects such as the production of metals and dyes, mathematics, some of these dating to 1800-1600 B.C. The Chinese developed a sophisticated civilization far back in ancient times, a full documentary study of all branches of science, technology, chemistry, biology, agriculture and medicine. Early Egyption papyrus reveal a scientific interest in subjects such as the production of metals and dyes, mathematics and veterinary medicine. The most complete scientific writings are from ancient Greece. The Arabs also contributed much literature in the fields of medicine, astronomy, mathematics, chemistry, physics etc. It was the invention of printing in the 15th century, which made the wide and rapid diffusion of knowledge possible. Thus, it is one of the most significant developments both in the history of science and in the history of research and technical libraries.

The proliferation of private materials promoted the establishment of various early private collections. Examples are the astronomy collection of Conrad Gesher (1516-1565) and the collection of Dr. John Dee (1527-1608), mainly consisting of works of medieval science. Various scientists maintained large collections. Among these were the collections of Sir Charles Scarburgh, M.D. (1616-1694), Robert Boyle (1627-1691), Robert Hooke (1635-1703), Edward Bernard (1638-1696), Sir Isaac Newton (1642-1727), Martin Folkes (1690-1754), Carl Linnaeus (1707-1778) and enormous. Later private collections of note included that of Benjamin Franklin (1706-1790), a natural history collection of Sir Joseph Banks (1743-1820), the collection of Nathaniel Bowitch (1773-1838), mainly devoted to mathematics and astronomy, the collection of Charles Darwin (1809-1882); John Thomas Groves (1806-1870) and Francis Joseph Cole (1872-1959) is devoted to an important Zoology collection.

Another significant development in the history of scientific/research and technical libraries was the rise of scientific societies. These societies were instrumental in the creation of experimental science. These modern scientific societies were the schools of ancient Greece (such as the schools of Thales, Pythagoras and Plato) and the museums and libraries of Alexandria founded by the Ptolemies. These schools resurfaced in the 16th century in Italy. Another important academy was founded in 1652, the Academia Naturae Curiosorum, which fueled the growth of science in the German states. One of the most important academies was the Royal Society founded in 1662 in London.

The publication of the various proceedings of these scientific societies gave birth to another significant development in the history of scientific and technical libraries- the growth of periodical literature. The first literature such as Philosophical Transactions of the Royal Society was published in 1665. By the end of the 18th century; however the scientific and technical journals have been sponsored and published by a variety of sources. With the advent of advanced technology in the mid-20th century, this development also lead towards library automation. In the last 20 years, computers have been more and more widely used for information storage and retrieval, particularly in science and technology. Today an appreciable number of scientific and technical journals, reports books etc, are available in both print and non-print forms.

History of research and technical libraries is the history of specialized institutions as R&T libraries are not the independent institutions. They are the components of specialized institutions such as government departments, scientific research and development centers, business and industrial undertaking, professional association, learned societies and institutions etc. The development of specialized institutions started in the 18th century with the development of the learned societies. The establishment and development R&T libraries in advanced countries is linked with industrial growth obtained primarly by application of scientific knowledge.

After World War-II, there was tremendous increase in the budgets for Research and development. Research and Technical library movement grew rapidly in various countries.

3.2 HISTORY AND DEVELOPMENTS OF R&T LIBRARIES WITH SPECIAL REFERENCE TO U.K, U.S.A. AND INDIA.

3.2.1 Historical Background and Developments In U.K.

The establishment of research and technical libraries in advanced countries is linked with industrial growth obtained primarily by application of scientific knowledge. The beginning of technical libraries in U.K. can be traced to private effort. Today, it is the government alongwith industries that are major sponsors of the technical library service. The development process of R&T libraries started in 18th century in the wake of establishment of scientific societies. The British Museum was founded in 1753. The concept of R&T libraries was established in the 19th and 20th century with the emergence of large number of scientific institutions, societies, national laboratories, trade associations etc. Some of the prominent 19th century institutions are the Institute of Civil Engineering (1818), Royal Astronomical Society (1824), Chemical Engineering (1841), Institute of Mechanical Engineering (1847), Institute of Electrical Engineers (1871), Science Museum Library (1883) etc. Some notable 20th century public and private institutions are the British Library, National Reference and Information Centre for Science and Technology, British Electrical and Applied Industrial Research Association, Patent office library, National Chemical Laboratory, Railway Technical Research Institute, Institute of Physics, Research Institute for National Defence, Plastics and Rubber Institute, the National Institute of Economic and Social Research is Britain's longest established independent economic research institute with over 60 years experience of applying academic excellence of the needs of business and policy makers. It was founded on 2nd June 1938, after a first initiative by Sir Josiah Stamp in the early 1930's and was incorporated under the Companies Act 1929.

3.2.1.1 Role of the British Museum Library

The British Library has played a significant role in the promotion, organization and dissemination of information supporting research and development. It deals with the information sources in the fields of natural sciences, technology, commerce and industry. The British library has four principal divisions under the chief executive:-

a) Humanities and Social-Sciences.

b) Science, Technology and Industry.

c) Bibliographic Service Division.

d) Research and Development Department.

The Science, Technology and Industry division has two main organs that is the British Library Science Reference and Information Service and British Document Supply Centre.

3.2.1.2 ASLIB: The Association for Information Management

The national professional association of special libraries in UK known as ASLIB was established in 1924 and is the second biggest association of special libraries in the world. Earlier the acronym ASLIB stood for Association of Special Libraries and Information Bureaux. ASLIB has a membership exceeding 3,000 spread over 70 countries i.e U.K with 80% and other countries 20% approximately. ASLIB promotes the study of documentation, librarianship and training for librarianship. ASLIB' major services include consultancy, research for industry and commercial organizations. It has a panel of translators who translates scientific papers covering principal countries of British Commonwealth.

3.2.2 Historical Background And Developments In USA

The concept of specialized service in U.S.A. owes its origin to the Public libraries. In 1731 the Library Corporation of Philadelphia, a group of librarians, considered providing special services in public libraries.

Until World War-I, there were only a few special libraries. Later, the industrial development and the need to meet America's military requirements paved way for the tremendous growth of R&T libraries. The USA today ranks among the most advanced nations in the field of science and technology and provides a wide base for information support to its scientific and social institution through libraries, information centres and systems. The USA today has not only the world's largest public library-The Library of Congress (LC) with millions of books and other material especially in social-sciences, history and geography but also special libraries in science and Technology such as the Atomic Research Library, Space Science Library, library of American Chemical Society, Bio-Sciences, Information service, library etc. Every Ministry of the Government, R&D units, banks and other major public and private institutions have their libraries providing specialized services. Besides this various professional associations and societies such as the National Science Foundation (NSF) (1952), Special Library Association (SLA) (1909), and American Society for Information Science (ASIS) (1966) have established their own libraries thereby playing a lead role in ensuring access to scientific information.

3.2.2.1 NSF : National Science Foundation

National Science Foundation (NSF) started

functioning in 1952 and played a lead role in ensuring access to scientific information. The NSF's major activities included the establishment of a committee for development of science information centers. The main objectives of NSF are as under:-

- To interchange scientific information among scientists of USA and other countries,
- To publish material on science & technology,
- To arrange symposia and seminars at international level,
- To translate work of scientific and technical books from other countries,
- To study the method and procedure for getting information for industrial organizations and defence laboratories and
- Aid various indexing and abstracting journals.

3.2.2.2 *SLA : Special Library Association*

SLA was established in 1909 and is the 2nd largest Association in USA after the American Library Association (ALA) and is the third largest in the world after ALA and Library Association (LA) of U.K. SLA membership is open to individual, institutions, societies, business and industrial organizations, educational and technical institutions, museums, newspaper libraries etc, and is working for their betterment in the areas of communication and resource utilization, SLA has undertaken various professional development programmes such as career advisory service and continuing education courses to meet the changing requirements of the profession.

3.2.2.3 *ASIS :American Society for Information Science*

It is one of the major organizations for the development of information transfer. It was established in 1926 and was named as ADI (American Documentation

Institute). ADI was named as ASIS in 1968. The ASIS focuses its attention on organizing, retrieving, disseminating and using information. It is based on information analysis, education for information survey, classification research, library automation, networks, reprographic technology, biomedical information etc.

3.2.3 Historical Background and Development in India

India is a vast country, rich in technical libraries which may be divided into three categories, Government and Semi-Government, technical libraries in Universities and other teaching institutions and those attached to Research Institutions and Societies. The development of specalised institutions started with the development of the learned societies came into existence with the initiative of Sir William Jones who visited India in 1783. He was a judge in the High Court. Apart from his judicial duties he used to take interest in scholarly activities such as organization of special books at local centre, seminars and setting up of learned societies. In 1784 Asiatic Society of Bombay. In the 19th century Calcutta became the earliest active centre for scientific research. Further, other societies namely Mathematical Society of India, Chemical Society of India, Astronomical Society of India etc. came into existence. Further some organisation came into existence such as Zoological Survey of India, Botanical Survey of India, Geological Survey of India, etc. These societies and organizations were founded with the donations given by the rich people. Several Indian Scientists such as J.C. Bose, C.V. Raman, Mahenderpal Sarkar, Raja Ram Mohan Roy etc. made efforts to develop these societies and organizations. Latter on three major Research Institutes – the Indian Council of Agricultural Research, Indian Council of Medical Research and the Council of Scientific and Industrial Research, each possessing its own library came into existence. While ICAR and ICMR are devoted to

Agriculture and medicine respectively, the CSIR is mainly concerned with the promotion of science, technology and industry of the country.

To serve the information needs of the 1.5 million scientific and technical personnel in the country, over 800 scientific and technical libraries exist with a collection of more than 10,000 volumes. Among them, the following are specifically worth noting:-

- The National Science Library of NISCAIR
- The National Medical Library of Ministry of Health.
- Defence Science Library of DESIDOC.
- National Medical Library, Delhi.

Some of the research organizations which are well developed to serve the information requirements of the users are as under :-

3.2.3.1 ISALIC (Indian Association of Special Library and Information Centres)

The ISALIC is an association of special libraries and information centres in India, which was formed in 1955 at Calcutta. Its main objective is to encourage and promote the systematic acquisition, organisation and dissemination of knowledge. It acts as a centre for research for special libraries and deals with documentation techniques, reprography and translation services in scientific, technical and other fields for 'researchers. It also publishes a directory of special and research libraries.

3.2.3.2 NISCAIR (National Institute of Science Communication and Information Resource)

The NISCAIR formerly known as INSDOC was established in 1952 at New Delhi. NISCAIR is a premier organization serving the information needs of scientific community by providing high quality information services based on recorded human knowledge of the world.

NISCAIR is engaged in providing S&T information and documentation services through various activities such as abstracting and indexing, design and development of databases, translation and reprographic service, library automation, providing access to international information sources, human resource development, consultancy services in setting up modern library-cum- information centre. NISCAIR's National Science Library (NSL) acts as a major information resource centre in the country in the area of S&T. NSL has a rich collection of over 2,00,000 volumes including monographs and bound volumes of journal in most of the fields of Science & Technology. It also publishes Indian Science Abstract.

3.2.3.3 DESIDOC (Defence Science Information Documentation Centre)

Realising the importance of special library set-up for the information needs of the Defence Science, the DRDO (Defence Research and Development Organisation) created a Scientific Information Bureau (SIB) in 1958 in Delhi. In 1967,SIB was reorganized and renamed as Defence Scientific Information and Documentation. DESIDOC provides, information services to India's defence establishments, among these services are collection publication of various science journals, prepares bibliographies, translation of defence articles published in foreign languages, reprographic service, CAS and SDI services. Defence Science Library (DSL) is one of the largest libraries having a unique collection of publications in various subjects such as S&T including aerospace, missiles, explosives, physical and life-sciences etc. DSL has a rich collection of 2,62,000 documents and provides document supply quite fast usually within 48 hours from its collection. More than 500 DRDO Scientists and few others are provided fortnightly and monthly current awareness services.

Someother prominent documentation centers are the Small Enterprises National Documentation Centre (SENDOC), the Social Science Documentation Centre (SSDC) and National Social Science Documentation Centre (NASSDOC).

3.2.3.4 NISSAT (National Information System for Science and Technology)

The NISSAT commenced its operations in 1997 with the objective of organizing information support facilities for a customer base largely dominated by people engaged in research and academics. The NISSAT programme has the mandate to cover the entire spectrum of science and technology. NISSAT has set up about 11 sectoral centers which are usually built around the existing information resources and facilities. They maintain extensive collections of published and unpublished documents in form of books, periodicals, R&D reports, technical reports, standards, patents and trade literature in their subject areas. NISSAT has initiated National Information Centers in the various subject areas such as Leather technology, food technology, machine tools production and engineering, drug and pharmaceuticals, textile and allied subjects, chemical and allied industries, management sciences, marine and aquatic sciences.

Besides providing documents and preparing bibliographies on request, they offer Selective Dissemination of Information (SDI), Current Awareness Service (CAS), reprographic and micrographic services, industrial and technical enquiry services, technical translation and similar access-delivery services.

3.2.3.5 ICSSR (Indian Council of Social Science Research)

The ICSSR was set up in 1960's at New Delhi to promote Social Science research. ICSSR conducts surveys from time to time to know the areas covered under research. It provides financial support to increase the quality and quantity of research projects in social sciences. ICSSR maintains data of research projects submitted to ICSSR to provide the information to the social scientists. The data is also converted in machine readable data base. It also organizes various conferences and seminars from time to time at national and international level. ICSSR has six regional centres in different regions were the researchers can use the library facility including document supply service, translation facility etc.

3.2.3.6 *BARC (Bhabha Atomic Research Centre)*

The department of Atomic Energy is one of the major scientific institutions in India. The BARC has a sophisticated library and information services division, which houses a large collection of Nuclear Literature including 3 lakh research reports.

3.2.3.7 *GSI (Geological Survey of India)*

GSI was established in 1851, is a government organisation in India for conducting geological surveys and studies. It is one of the oldest organizations in the world. The activities of the GSI was expanded to cover a broader geological study and studies of the earth sciences of India.

3.2.3.8 *Zoological Survey of India.*

Zoological Survey of Indian was established in 1916 to promote the survey, exploration and research of animals in the region.

Besides the above organizations National Medical Library in Delhi, collects medical literature from all over the world and publishes the Index to Indian Medical Periodicals. The Indian Agricultural Research Institute (IARI) Library in Delhi has excellent reprographic facilities and publishes the Indian Bibliography of Agriculture. The Council of Scientific and Industrial Research (CSIR) was established in 1969 and has a huge collection of technical literature.

CONCLUSION

It can be concluded that Information is recognized as an indispensable part for research and development. The post-independence period in India as well as other countries had witnessed the establishment of various bibliographical and documentation information centers for the promotion and development of scientific and technical research, thereby having strong base of research and technical libraries. The R&T libraries are well developed to meet the information requirements of its users.

4

Role of Research and Technical Libraries in Knowledge Society

4.1 INTRODUCTION

Libraries are recognized as repository of information and knowledge and an integral part of education, society and research. It is a social organization, effectively planned and organized for transmitting and accumulating experience of society to individual members of the society through society, to individual members of the society through books and other graphic materials like maps, charts, microfilms etc.

A research and technical library is the life blood of research organizations as well as professional bodies and learned societies. The basic information role of the R&T libraries is to collect the materials containing the information required by the various sections of the society and disseminate the information to them through appropriate methods.

R&T libraries are indispensable for society. These

educate, inform and convert an individual into a better citizen. It makes information available in a better, organized and more economical manner. The purpose of research and technical libraries is to expand the horizons of knowledge for socio-economic advancement which in turn depends upon the progress in scientific and technological fields. Access to existing knowledge and information is essential for research. The knowledge that is newly created is communicated through the media of journals, research reports and other similar publications. Every R&T library attached to an institution engaged in research should have a strong collection of publications to support research programmes.

4.2 RESEARCH AND TECHNICAL LIBRARY AS A PART OF EDUCATION

Research and Technical libraries occupies an important role in the modern educational system. Its aim is to educate the researchers for their higher studies and to provide opportunities for continuing education to the educated. Today research is more library oriented and library centered. Researchers need information continuously and are considered to be the largest users of libraries. To provide the society with competent men and women trained in agriculture, arts, medicine, industry, science and technology and various other professions research and technical libraries are needed. Due to inter-disciplinary and multi-disciplinary nature of research, the research and technical libraries have crossed their boundaries. The present communication technologies have given a new approach to the research libraries to justify its existence in the knowledge society. In this context the following points are discussed.

* **Disseminating Humantarian Information**

A wealth of essential humanitarian information is produced by various international organizations, such as the United Nations, UNESCO; WHO and various other national organizations. This information is made freely available in the form of networked research and technical libraries.

* **Disaster Relief**

Natural disaster such as earthquakes, storms, floods, hurricanes etc. demand immediate information. Disaster relief situations are complex and in such situation Research and Technical libraries play an important role in disseminating immediate information so that relief services can be provided effectively and efficiently.

* **Preserving Culture**

Research and Technical libraries have always been involved in preserving culture. The Research and Technical libraries can acquire and preserve literature and artifacts and use them to disseminate knowledge and understanding of different cultures.

* **Locally Produced Information**

In Research and Technical libraries there are countless number of locally produced information collections. Scientists prepare research report materials that addresses specific community problems and adapt some of them which are based on unpublished local information material. Indigenous people have invaluable medicinal knowledge based on local plants or long acquired knowledge of the cultivation and protection of local species. Such knowledge is of vital use and more than half of the world's most frequently prescribed drugs are derived from plants and this trend of information is growing.

4.3 RESEARCH AND TECHNICAL LIBRARIES IN KNOWLEDGE BASED SOCIETY

Knowledge plays an important role in the development of society throughout history. The transformation of information and knowledge society has largely been brought about as a result of the accumulation of knowledge and the advances in information and communication technologies. Knowledge belongs to the individual and on it depends other forms of knowledge including information.

The human society is widely responsible for growth and development of all kinds of knowledge which overflow through the minds of common people. A society plays a significant role in developing various branches of knowledge and putting them together for better use. The society has always remained a vital force behind the emergence and development of new aspects of knowledge. Knowledge and society are inter-linked and inter-dependent. The developments in knowledge are closely associated with the developments in the societies. Today, a society that consumes a minimum of knowledge and information is the least developed society. Research and Technical library is one of the agencies that plays an important role in the spread of knowledge. To facilitate the easy transfer and dissemination of information, it acts as an intermediary between the creator and consumer of information. So it is necessary for the society to come forward in a big way to strengthen and smoothen the functioning of the library by organizing the entire universe of knowledge.

The social role of research and technical library is very complex and the responsibilities which the society has placed upon it is very heavy. The R&T libraries plays an important role in knowledge society. To serve as a social agency the R&T library has to play the following role in the growth of knowledge:

- It helps to assemble, organize, preserve, socialize and serve the growing knowledge embodied in growing number of books, periodicals and several types of graphic materials such as maps, charts, micro-films, micro-fiche, audio-visual aids etc.
- It helps in transmission of knowledge from earlier generation to latter ones,
- It helps in further building of knowledge from generation to generation,
- It helps in the contemporary development of knowledge, by the purposeless repetition of effort and wastage in the research potential of humanity,
- It helps to conserve the research time of humanity.

4.4 KNOWLEDGE SOCIETY AND INFORMATION TECHNOLOGY

A sea-change is taking place in all aspects of human society. The recent developments in Science and Technology has led to a new alarming situation regarding knowledge created in the world. There has been amazing and spectacular developments in the access and availability of information and knowledge. The chief driving force of this development is Information Technology. Knowledge and information can be accessed today instantly, irrespective of its location and made available on a computer screen, downloaded and stored for future use. The science and technology has always benefited us with its gifts among which Information Technology is the leading and advancing technology in today's life. For this purpose application of IT in R&T libraries requires to be done at a very rapid speed so that new knowledge which is created is disseminated at the global level within no time.

In a society which is becoming increasingly influenced

by computers, telecommunication, micrography, information storage and media technologies, it is recognized that users need the facility interacting with the new technology, as soon as possible. Digital technology has influenced all aspects of human life. The technology today has changed the print media in digital media. At present knowledge is not only confined to books and periodicals but it is available in various electronic forms such as floppy disks, microfiches, microfilms, magnetic disks, DVD's, CD-ROM's etc. which has directly revolutionized the functioning of R&T libraries.

CONCLUSION

Thus, Research and Technical libraries and society are inter-linked and inter-department. Society without libraries has no significance and libraries without society has no origin. Today we look upon R&T library as a social agency. It is from the very beginning that the R&T libraries has been a product of social organization. It has been created by actual necessities in modern civilization. It is a product of society for its cultural advancement and plays a vital role in the conservation, extension (research) and transmission (teaching) of knowledge.

5

Resource Sharing in Research and Technical Libraries

5.1 INTRODUCTION

Invention of printing press, opening of more and more academic and research institutions, spread of education and technological advances are some of the factors which have lead to exponential growth of literature. These days millions of micro and macro-documents and other documents are brought out in different countries of the world in several languages and on all possible subjects every year. It has been estimated that about 3000 pages or 250 million words are being printed every minute at the global level. The growth rate of knowledge in Science and Technology is doubling in every two years than that of Social-Sciences. The growth rate of publication of books and journals especially in the field of Science and Technology is almost three times greater than that of the growth rate of world population. According to one estimate, the number of scientific periodicals was about 100 in 1800, 500 by 1830, 1000 by 1850, 10,000 by 1900 and 1 lakh by 1950 and now it is almost 10 times more than it was in the 20th century. Thus, the growth rate of information is faster than ever before and it is still accelerating. In such a situation it becomes unrealistic even for the biggest library to acquire all possible documents or all the print or non-print materials required by it users, because of physical and financial crises. It is for this reason that someone has suggested that the slogan "No library can stand alone" should be adopted as the sixth law of library science.

5.2 DEFINITION

Resource Sharing in Research and Technical library is one of the most important concepts and therefore, document delivery is the principal activity involved in it. Resource Sharing in the libraries not only enhances the use and utilization of library resources and services but also ensures optimum benefits to their users in the utilization of library resources of all kinds. It not only serves to effect economy in terms of time and money but also ensures much better services to the users.

The word Resource -Sharing can be analysed as follows:-

Resources - All sort of documents/ resources of the library.

Sharing - To be participated in sharing of the resources.

That is "All sort of documents/resources of the library to be participated in sharing of the resources."

Hence in the context of libraries the resource sharing means sharing of resources among the libraries based on the agreement between them. The resources may be the staff, equipment, money and collection. The term library co-operation used by library professionals for a long-time, was latter on changed and was termed as Resource-Sharing.

According to Allen Kent, resource sharing is a "mode of operations whereby the library functions are shared in common by all members of the cooperating libraries," and has identified four basic facets of resource sharing that is

- Acquisition.
- Processing.
- Storage
- Delivery of Services.

Kent considers these facets as the primary objectives of "this unique concept".

5.3 NEED OF RESOURCE SHARING

The main factors that necessitate adoption of resource sharing among research and technical libraries.

5.3.1 Literature Explosion

Due to literature explosion information is growing at a very high rate and this has made it impossible for a library to attain self-sufficiency. Therefore resources sharing is necessary.

5.3.2 Readers Demand

There had been tremendous increase in the number of users of a library and their varied demands. The advancements in the entire field of knowledge and inter-disciplinary approach in education have resulted in diversified demands by various sections of researchers to quench their thirst of knowledge and information needs.

5.2.3 Limited Resources And Space

A single library is not capable of meeting all the requirements of its clientele/users. Limited resources of libraries in terms of money, space and manpower also stress upon the need for resource sharing. Even the most resourceful library of the most advanced country can not afford to acquire, organize and put to use all the materials that may be required by its users. Due to increasing cost of documents, it is very difficult for the research and technical libraries to acquire all the relevant documents. Apart from finance, a library's space is also limited. Due to lack of sufficient space for placing the huge collection, research and technical libraries have to depend upon the other libraries to meet the information requirements of the users. Similarly a library cannot employ any number of staff to organize and put to use unlimited numbers of documents because staff, like books and other documents require both finance and space.

5.4 PREREQUISITES / BASIC REQUIREMENTS OF RESOURCE SHARING.

Following are the basic requirements/ prerequisites of resource sharing :-

5.4.1 Agreement Among Library Authorities:-

For resource sharing, the participating libraries should agree on the following basic issues:-

a) The participating libraries should agree to share all resources they have. There should be clear cut terms and conditions defined to avoid administrative complicacies.

b) There should be a written agreement on division of responsibilities on acquisition.

c) There should be an agreement on document description also. If all the participating libraries in the system, agree to follow the same classification scheme and cataloguing code, shared cataloguing then resource sharing will be flexible.

d) There should also be an agreements in respect of some details, like loan period, payment for loss of materials etc.

5.4.2 Union Catalogue

If the participating libraries have once agreed on the above issues, the stage has been set for the resource sharing. After setting the system of resource sharing among the research and technical libraries, the immediate problem that arises upon them, is how to know that which library is having a particular document. For all this the R&T libraries of the system may be tried until the document is found. The process is time and labour consuming, which should be avoided and an alternative is to compile a union-catalogue within all R&T Libraries.

5.4.3 Computerized Library Network

The use of computer and library networking have given resource sharing a new direction. The concept has been strengthened with the IT support and networking of libraries at local, national and international levels has made it possible to know instantly the holdings of other participating libraries in the system.

5.5 METHODS OF RESOURCE SHARING.

Following are two methods of resource sharing:-

1. Conventional Resource Sharing.
2. Non-Conventional Resource sharing.

5.5.1 Conventional Resource Sharing

Under this method the libraries participate in the traditional ways such as inter-library loan, inter-library study facility, compilation of traditional tools, cooperative acquisition programme, cooperative storage programme etc. Mostly the libraries of less developed and underdeveloped countries follow the conventional method of resource sharing.

5.5.2 Non-Conventional Resource Sharing

Under this method/programme the libraries

participate under resource sharing programme through the application of computers, lazers, micrographies, setting up of computer data-bases etc. This method is being used only by the developed countries. The under developed countries cannot think of shifting to non-conventional methods due to lack of financial resources, lack of development of latest technology, due to lack of suitable environment etc.

5.6 RESOURCE SHARING IN RESEARCH & TECHNICAL LIBRARIES

There is no define agreement for resource-sharing among research and technical libraries in India. A number of methods are adopted by the R&T libraries in India which are as under:-

5.6.1 Inter Library Loan (ILL)

It is the most common method used in research and technical libraries in India. R&T libraries functioning under the administrative control of a Central Council share their documents on ILL bases. For example - Libraries of CSIR laboratories, medical libraries, agricultural libraries, atomic energy establishment etc. The items which are not considered for loans generally include bulky items, fragile material prone to adverse effect by careless handling, documents currently in demands, confidential nature of material, reference material, bound volume of a set of journals, or a particular volume of a set of journals, multi-volume books, micro-films etc. DELNET maintains an online Union Catalogue of books available in its member-libraries. The request for ILL can be placed through the online system.

5.6.2 Collection Development through Exchange Basis

R & T libraries in India are developing their collection particularly research journals, on exchange basis. For example - NISCAIR's, National Science Library subscribes only about its 1/3rd of its journals and rest are acquired through exchange. Likewise Indian National Science Academic Library Delhi receives about 1500 current journals annually only about 250 journals are subscribed and the rest are received on the exchange basis.

5.6.3 Compilation of Information Tools

Various R&T Libraries compile the information tools on cooperative basis. NISCAIR and NASSDOC, the national documentation centres for sciences and social sciences respectively, have brought out a number of union catalogues of periodicals and serials with the help of participating libraries. Another major institution which has brought out union catalogues is the Defence Research and Development Organization (DRDO). Its Union Catalogue of Periodicals in DRDO libraries in two volumes covers 6000 periodicals, including proceedings, transactions and bulletins of learned bodies. Agricultural libraries maintain a Union Catalogue of the dissertations available in these libraries. IIT's Indian Institute of Technology and IISc, Indian Institute of Science maintain a catalogue of their holding, Some national level organizations responsible for the administration of special libraries such as UGC and CSIR compile a directory of ongoing research projects.

5.6.4 Translation

Scientific information is available in number of languages of nations which have made tremendous scientific and economic advances. The availability of translations, is reported by the World Translations Index, a monthly publication covering largely science and technology and briefly social sciences. The online DIALOG file of the World Translations Index contains nearly two Lac citation and annual updating of about 30,000 records. The documentation centres in countries like Denmark, France, Germany, Greece, Holland, India, Spain, Switzerland, U.K.

etc provide translations on request.

5.7 RESOURCE SHARING AND NETWORKING IN R&T LIBRARIES

The concept of library co-operation and resource sharing in research and technical libraries has been strengthened with the IT support and networking of libraries at local, national and international level is gaining momentum. The resource sharing networks provide services such as bibliographical information, factual data, shared cataloguing like OCLC Network, Inter-library loan etc. The resource sharing network projects include the Bombay Library Network (BONET), Calcutta Library Network (CALIBNET), Developing Library Network (DELNET), Madras Library Network (MALIBNET), Pune Library Network (PUNENET) etc. There are also various national information networks in designated fields such as ERNET, INFLIBNET, NICNET etc.

5.7.1 Developing Library Network (DELNET)

DELNET has been established with the prime objective of promoting resource sharing among the libraries through the development of a network of libraries. It has been actively engaged with the compilation of various Union catalogues of the resources available in member libraries. It has already created the Union Catalogue of Books, Union list of Current Periodicals. Union Catalogue of Periodicals, CD-ROM databases, databases of Indian Specialists, Database of Periodicals articles, Union list of Video Recordings, Urdu Manuscripts database, database of theses and dissertations and several other databases.

5.7.2 Pune Libraries Networking Project (Pune Net)

Pune Net is a joint programme of the University of Pune, the centre for development of Advanced Computing (C-DAC) and the National Chemical Laboratory (NCL). The project is funded by National Information System for Science and Technology (NISSAT) of the department of Scientific and Industrial Research (DSIR), Government of India. The Pune Library Networks aims at sharing of resources by creating databases and communication between libraries of the Poona metropoliation area.

5.7.3 Information Library Network (INFLIBNET)

Inflibnet is a major national programme initiated by the UGC in 1991 with its Head Quarters at Gujarat University Campus (Ahmedabad). INFLIBNET is aimed at providing channel for academicians and resources for exchange of information from sources within the country and abroad. The network is known as INFLIBNET, an information and library network. The UGC described the INFLIBNET as co-operative network which would contribute to sharing and utilization of resources, facilities and services of libraries and information centres in the university system as well as in the R&D organizations. It is a national network interconnecting various libraries and information centres in the country. It helps to optimize information resource utilization through shared cataloguing and inter-library loan service. It encourages co-operation among libraries, documentation centres and information centres in the country, so that the resources can be accessed for the benefit of helping the weaker resource centres by stronger ones.

5.7.4 National Information System for Science and Technology (NISSAT)

National Information System for Science and Technology has taken initiatives for promoting resource sharing activities aimed to ensure better utilization of information resources. Besides the development of library, network, its programmes also included preparation of Union Catalogues.

5.7.5 Education and Research Network (ERNET)

The ERNET has been established by the Department of Electronics with funding support from the Government of India and United Nations Development Programme for linking computing resources available at the Indian Institute of Science, Bangalore, National Centre for Software Technology, Mumbai and the Indian Institutes of Technology at Delhi, Mumbai, Chennai, Kanpur and Khargpur. It is the first and important network in the country in the field of education and research. The main emphasis of this network to the community is relationship with research and development, establishment of other networks and the functions for creating interactive cooperation. For performing the functions, the facilities being provided by ERNET network to the users of the country are joint product development, technology transfer consultancy services, education and training facilities. And for arranging these functions ERNET has done the provision of various services such as Electronic Mail Service, File transfer service, Remote log on, bibliographic database access, audio and audio-plus conferencing and bulletin board service.

5.7.6 INDONET

INDONET is an integrated information management and distributed data processing facility. It is a commercial network with nodes at Kolkata, Mumbai and Chennai. It is also connected to other cities like the Ahmedabad, Bangalore Delhi and Pune. This network helps in the export of software and have a distributed data processing system. Its aim is to process large amount of scientific and industrial data centrally and efficiently and provide access to remote user terminals.

5.7.7 NICNET (National Informatics Centre Network)

NICNET was established in 1977 as an Information

network by National Information Centre. It is established as a main national information system for the transmission dissemination and communication of information, which is based on multiple access technique and uses c-200 series micro-earth station. Several information systems have been established and developed which disseminate the required information to the users. They are Accounts and Budget, Loan Planning, Customs and Central Excise, Import/Export distribution, Estate Duty, Media, Forestry and Wildlife, Economics and Social Themes, Health, Education, Water and Irrigation, Rural Development, Transport Industry, Small-scale Industries, Construction Industries, Mines and Minerals, Tourism and Management.

5.7.8 SIRNET (Scientific and Industrial Research Network)

Scientific and Industrial Research Network is a computer communication network initially started for CSIR Laboratories. The SIRNET mail node is at INSDOC and is connected to Education and Research Network (ERNET) set up by Department of Electronics (DOE). The software used for SIRNET is Basic Networking Software with standard UNIX package to communicate with other UNIX systems.

5.7.9 ADINET (Ahmedabad Library Network)

ADINET is a network of libraries located in and around Ahmedabad established with the sponsorship of NISSAT. Its aim is to integrate the economic, scientific and technical information systems into an effective network in and around Ahmedabad; to facilitate and promote sharing of resources amongst the libraries and information centers in and around Ahmedabad by developing and maintaining a central online union catalogue containing bibliographic information on books, serials and non-book materials of all the participating libraries. Various services offered by ADINET are online information, interlibrary loan, photocopying service, CAS, information service and internet service.

5.7.10 BONET (Bombay Library Network)

BONET offers simplified accessing to enormous and comprehensive collections and services by offering links to all academic and R&D libraries in and around Mumbai. Its aim is to make information available to researchers at low cost, using computer networking facilities and at the same time enhancing inter-library cooperation. Various services offered by BONET are an online catalogue of periodicals named as Unicat, access to online information on books in member libraries, inter-library lending service for books and periodicals, inter-library request service for photocopying, an online information retrieval system for computer science and software technology, online access to foreign library catalogues and online access to commercial databases such as DIALOG.

5.7.11 MYLIBNET (Mysore Library Network)

MYLIBNET was established at Mysore city in the year 1995 and the Central Food Technology Research Institute (CFTRI), Mysore being an active member of Mysore City Library Consortium (MCLC), is hosting this network in its premises. The main objective of MYLIBNET is to prepare a union catalogue of periodicals subscribed by the member libraries. In order to have faster communication among libraries, MYLIBNET has been subscribing to electronic mail service of Education and Research Network (ERNET) of Department of Electronics Govt. of India.

5.7.12 UGC-INFONET: (University Grants Commission-Information Network)

In order to bring a qualitative change in the academic infrastructure especially for higher Education, University Grants Commission has took an initiative in modernizing the University Campuses with state of the-art campus wide networks and setting up its own nationwide communication network named as UGC-Infonet. It is a tool to distribute education material and journals to the remotest of areas and a resource for researchers and scholars for tapping the most up-to-date information. It acts as a channel for Globalization of Education and facilitates the universities in marketing their services and developments.

5.7.13 INTERNET

Internet is a network of thousands of networks providing its users access to the world information in various fields. It is a worldwide web of interconnected university, business, military and science networks and is made up of Local Area Network (LAN's), Metropolitan Area Network (MAN's) and huge Wide Area Networks (WAN's) connecting computers for organizations in the world. The internet connecting nearly 50,000 networks in about 80 countries can be accessed by 20 million people around the world for various Internet service including electronic mail (e-mail), file - transfer, conferencing and database services, bulletin board service etc.

5.8 Merits of Resource Sharing

Following are the merits of resource sharing:-

5.8.1 Collection

Through resource sharing libraries develop a balanced collection in a particular area. In research and technical libraries most of the collection pertains to reference works, journals, patents, reports, indexes, abstracts, pamphlets conference proceedings etc. Participating libraries can join their resources and develop rich collection.

5.8.2 Equipment

The participating libraries can make use of the

equipment of other libraries. They can also get the benefit of various equipment, such as computers, micro-filming equipment, CD-ROM etc.

5.8.3 Elimation of Duplication

Resource sharing helps to eliminate duplication of processing work in libraries.

5.8.4 Economy

Overall library economy is achieved through resource sharing. It not only saves money, but manpower and machinery can be utilized for other services in the library.

5.8.5 Union Catalogue

The participating libraries can compile those information tools which are not available in the market such as directories, union catalogues etc.

5.8.6 Uniformity

Resource sharing ensures uniformity in internal and physical forms of catalogue among the participating libraries.

5.8.7 Quality

It ensures qualitative cataloguing and classification at cheaper cost because at selected places expert cataloguers are engaged for cataloguing books.

5.9 DEMERITS OF RESOURCES SHARING

Following are some of the disadvantages of Resource sharing:-

1. It gives rise to unemployment of classifiers and cataloguers because they will be required at the centralized or selected places mainly.
2. In case the centralized library or agency is not a copyright library, it becomes troublesome to operate

the scheme. Because in case the participating library acquires such a book which is not available with the centralized library, the participating library will either be required to process the book for itself or to send the book or details thereof to the central library. This process is time consuming.

3. Libraries adopting different forms and types of catalogue and different schemes of classification cannot participate in resource sharing programme.

CONCLUSION

Inspite of the efforts made by Research and Technical libraries for resource sharing the result is not as encouraging as it should have been. Various R&T libraries are acquiring the documents individually, so lot of duplication is found even among the neighbouring research and technical libraries. So there is no proper economic planning and utilization of library resources. Moreover the administrative barriers do not let research and technical libraries to participate in resource sharing programme.

6

Impact of Information Technology on Research and Technical Libraries

6.1 INTRODUCTION

The information explosion of recent years has led to the phenomenal increase in the production of scientific and technical literature. Approximately one million articles are published every year. The explosion of information keeps the budget of the library in a critical position. Librarians feel quite difficult to acquire relevant documents for their readers. Because of knowledge explosion, users have been confronted with the problems of searching and retrieving the required information in right time. The storage and maintenance of huge information on paper documents have become extremely costly, time consuming and labour intensive. However, the present society, requires pinpointed, exhaustive and expeditious information centers. Therefore, to keep the pace with the information explosion, the information centers have to use the modern technologies. Today innovations in computer and telecommunications technology have resulted in major changes in basic library operations.

The term Information Technology (IT) is most commonly used which means a combination of computer and communication technologies used for information storage, retrieval and dissemination. According to **ALA Glossary** information technology is the application of computers and other technologies to the acquisition, organization, storage retrieval and dissemination of information. Information technology is a product of information science and technology. The word **'Information Technology'** is a combination of two words. One is 'Information' and the other is 'Technology'. Information means knowledge, it can be a bit or a para or a page is the systematic applications of scientific and other organized knowledge, skills to practical tasks by use of computer and communication.

6.2 NEED FOR INFORMATION TECHNOLOGY

To cope up with the increase and demand for scientific and technical information, the government, research, scientific and technical and industrial libraries began to explore and apply the technology of computers to library operations and to the development of machine readable bibliographical files. Computer has brought in a new impact to the library and information usage. It is widely used in the library's housekeeping operations which are of a repetitive nature.

Following are the factors which emphasize the need for automation:-

(i) Capacity to handle any amount of data/information.

(ii) Participating in networking programmes and resource sharing among libraries .

(iii) Flexibility in information search.

(iv) Standardization.

(v) Complexity and scattering information.

(vi) Literature explosion or information load.

(vii) Speedy processing of information and its retrieval.

(viii) Better bibliographic control at local/regional/ national/international level.

(ix) Interdisciplinary nature of research and information.

(x) Economic implication of new information technology.

(xi) Geographical and other barriers to communicate.

(xii) Increase in the number of users.

(xiii) Literature searching is cumbersome and time consuming.

(xiv) Non-availability of documents/information in the library.

(xv) Access to the information/data generated, but not published.

6.3 BASIC REQUIREMENTS FOR AUTOMATING A RESEARCH AND TECHNICAL LIBRARY

For the effective functioning of research and technical libraries, the following requisites are essential in respect of Information technology:-

- Adequate Collection,
- Financial Assistance,
- Computer Hardware,
- Library Software,
- Training of Staff,
- Users Education,
- Networking Facilities and co-operation,
- Maintenance and Development.
- Database creation.

6.3.1 Adequate Collection

Collection of a library forms the basis for library automation. Larger the collection the more is the need of automation to increase efficiency of the library services.

6.3.2 Financial Assistance

Computerization involves money. Sufficient funds are required for the establishment of computer systems, purchase of library software, training of staff, entry of library data and also for running the facility as a matter of routine work.

6.3.3 Computer Hardware

The selection of computer hardware for automation involves careful planning. There are many types of computers available in the market. The computer to be purchased for the library should meet the specific needs of the library. The technology is changing fast, therefore, the latest computers with adequate speed and memory should be acquired from the market.

6.3.4 Library Software

Library software activate computers to perform the desired functions. A large variety of library soft wares are available in the market. But the selection of software depends upon the nature of the library. The software which is used in Research and technical library should be user-friendly.

6.3.5 Training of Staff and Users Education

Designing of information systems for automation of Research and Technical libraries is a joint venture of librarians and software engineers. The librarians present their requirement into a logical order and the software engineers incorporate suitable provision to make the system work. Both of them analyze the same functions but their approaches are different. Now, the work of system designing has become easier with the availability of readymade software packages for automation of the Research and Technical libraries.

Library staff needs training in handling the computer hardware, software and for the performance of data entry work. Earlier it was a difficult task but with the advent of user-friendly software, the work on computer has been made simple. The training is generally provided by the hardware and software supplying agencies. Users also need training in retrieval. Users' education programmes are to be designed to educate the user about computerized databases, on-line searches, user-friendly systems. Training of staff in maintenance of the hardware and software is an essential part of the work of database creation. The hardware and software suppliers undertake to impart the working knowledge about their products.

6.3.6 Networking Facilities and Co-operation

Networking facilities and co-operation with other Research and Technical Libraries and databases is also required.

6.3.7 Maintenance and Development

During the use of computer there may be some disorder in computer hardware, software and databases. For this purpose, professionally trained staff with computer background are employed in R&T Libraries.

6.3.8 Database Creation

A database is a set of data that is related to each other. The advantages of computerized databases are many over the manual ones due to vast memory, speed and accuracy of computer which stores, processes and delivers information once fed into the desired sequences. The most time taking process in computerization is data entry. It needs the services of professionally trained library staff.

The best and the most appropriate source for data entry is the document. Being complete in itself, a document provides the maximum possible details. In some cases the body of the text is also consulted for bringing out the required information that is not available anywhere else. Every library maintains record of documents in a standardized format. The two broad categories of such records are Accession Registers and Catalogue Cards. All possible details about a particular document are copied in the accession register at the time of purchase. Every Research and technical library maintains catalogue cards of different categories like author, title, subject etc. It is the confidential record of library kept in the high security zone and maintained in a classified order. Various new methods of data entry have emerged with the advancement in the hardware and software. The catalogue of Library of Congress may be acquired on CD-ROM or online for transfer of the relevant entries to the developing database of the interested libraries. This allows speed and accuracy. Further, the data so entered is available in a standardized format which can be shared on national as well as international level.

Data in a computerized form is the end product of a long exercise and it works as a source for all the operations of the libraries. Such data on the disk of the computer system is always exposed to risk of viruses and other hazards. There are many reasons for loss of the entered data and the risk factor is comparatively higher in the environment of R&T libraries where suitably trained computer professionals are few in number and the systems are to be operated by many persons.

There are many methods of data security. The most common of them is its copying from time to time on floppies or CD's. Viruses generally come through floppies and CD's brought from outside or from the internet connections, therefore the use of such items should be avoided as for as possible. It should be made a regular exercise to run anti-virus software on the system to free disk from the viruses. Entry of unauthorized users can be restricted by incorporating provision of passwords for the hardware as well as software.

6.4 IMPACT OF IT ON HOUSE-KEEPING OPERATIONS AND SERVICES

Information technology enables libraries to provide most efficient and specialized information services. It has been fairly established that efficient information support and effective communication in organisation are closely associated with high performance, productivity and innovation. Computers can be used in performing most of the repetitive works of library in a desired number of times speedily and economically without wastage of time. Most of the operations within library are inter-related, inter-dependent and mutually supportive for the overall mission of library. Use of IT applications saves lot of staff time as the same data used is not to be entered at every stage.

Computer is used in various fields of library activities. Some of the areas of automation being used are like acquisition, technical processing, circulation control reference service and serial control. Automation has helped libraries in improving library operations and accelerating their working.

To cope up with increase in demand for scientific and technical information, the libraries began to explore and apply the technology of computers to library operations and to the development of machine readable files. Information Technology has brought out a new impact on Research and Technical libraries. The IT can be applied in the following areas in R&T libraries for performing house - keeping operations.

6.4.1 Acquisition

The computerized acquisition system has eased the burden for ordering of books, record checking of duplicate purchase orders and follow-up action can also be taken automatically. IT has speeded up the accessioning and other processing work of the acquisition section by eliminating large amount of repetitive and time-consuming operations. Selection of new books can be done from commercially available services which disseminate information about forthcoming documents, or directly from MARC tapes or any local inputs. Two files are maintained in a computer-based acquisitions system. The first file is the main file containing records of all current orders. The second file contains the names and addresses of booksellers used by the Library. A code number for each bookseller links the two files, so that bookseller information is not repeated in the order file. The system prints out the orders addressing the appropriate supplier. When the item is received in the library the order record with the bibliographic details becomes the basis of the catalogue record. The edited record is merely added to the catalogue file.

The other processes that can be performed by a computerized acquisition systems are:-

(i) Listing items on order by author, subject, title etc.

(ii) New accession listing and preparation of accession lists.

(iii) Payment of bills.

(iv) Transfer of details for classification and cataloguing.

6.4.2 Technical Processing/Cataloguing

Cataloguing includes the job of describing, recording and displaying details of the holdings of the library. Computers are used to aid in the production, maintenance and updating catalogue. It is used in maintaining bibliographic file consisting complete cataloguing elements as required by MARC, CCF etc, Authority control file, OPAC, shelf list, accession file. The other functions which are performed by a computerized technical processing system are :-

(i) Cataloguing of documents in accordance with the standard code of cataloguing.

(ii) Assignment of subject headings.

(iii) Preparation of book cards etc. used in circulation.

(iv) Feeding of class numbers and cataloguing details in computers.

(v) Retrospective conversion of records.

6.4.3 Circulation

Circulation of documents is one of the important house-keeping operations of a Research and Technical library. The automation of circulation function of a library is one of the most difficult tasks. This is because of complications involved in the procedure. Circulation procedure in a conventional system is very lengthy and consumes much of the staff time in respective works. The use of technological devices such as computers, barcode scanners, RFID technology etc. helps in the performance of the routine circulation operations easily and quickly. It saves lot of time of staff as well as users. It helps the library staff as well as of users. It helps the library staff in charging and discharging of documents, reservation of documents, sending reminders, collection of overdue, inter-library loan, maintenance of various records very quickly and efficiently.

6.4.4 Serial Control

Computers help in selection and acquisition, receipt and payment of journals, renewal of journals, checking in periodical collection and claiming missing issues, circulation of current issues, indexing of articles, verification of the cost and other details of journals through the list of publishers. It also helps in maintaining record of budget sanctioned and amount expended for different categories of serials.

6.4.5 Reference Service

Reference service is much more influenced by the developments in IT than any other services of library and information centres. Information technology reduces the response time for reference query. The major reference sources are readily available in optical discs as well as on-line databases and a lot of information can be searched by using the Internet resources. Computers also help in maintaining reference collection, prepare bibliographies for research workers and performs comprehensive literature search service by searching various information sources in print and non-print form within the library, outside the library or at national or international level, in a short time with accuracy. Other activities which are related to the reference service in library are :-

(i) Public access/ computer literacy.

(ii) Access to electronic databases available on CD-ROM's and Internet.

(iii) Providing selective dissemination of information and

(iv) Online Reference Service.

6.4.6 Office Automation/Management

Computers can be utilized effectively for office automation. Word processor makes typing, storing and editing jobs easier. Electronic mailing can reduce lot of effort in office work. Computer also helps in accounting and budgeting, and preparing statistics and annual reports. It helps in making policies for library service, preparing statement of expenditure that is total library budget, amount of funds received from other sources, statement of expenditure of the other funds and statements of expenditure of the last year.

6.4.7 Stock Verification

In R&T libraries, materials are shelved in sequences that is textbooks, general-books, reference collections, rare reserved and non-book materials. The users have free access to them in most of the cases due to open access system. As a result documents are displaced and also lost sometimes. To ascertain the loss and disorder, stock verification is carried out after certain intervals. Computerized Stock Verification involves the following functions :-

(i) Preparation of lists of acquired documents according to the accession numbers.

(ii) Comparison of the accession numbers of both the lists.

(iii) Listing of the documents not found in the issue record.

(iv) Listing of the lost documents.

For the above mentioned work, three computerized lists are obtained and one of them relates to the record of the missing ones.

6.4.8 Resource Sharing and Networking :

Computers help to undertake various resource-sharing and networking activities such as shared - cataloguing, on-line references, shared-circulation and on-line transmission of information are some of the services rendered by networks Co-ordination with other regional, national and international networks and libraries for exchange of documents and information is possible through on-line, e-mail and internet.

6.4.9 Information Storage/Retrieval :

Information storage/retrieval involves following functions :-

(i) Database construction,

(ii) Online database searching,

(iii) Indexing and abstracting,

(iv) Current Awareness Service.

(v) SDI Service.

(vi) Reprography Service.

Major computerized information services are CAS, SDI and Retrospective searches. The current awareness services are designed to provide information regarding current literature, generated through different sources received in the library. It helps the users to keep themselves up-to-date in the field of his work. The Selective Dissemination of Information is an extension of CAS. The method of automating the current awareness service is known as selective dissemination of information. SDI is a service that uses computers to enable current information occurring in variety of sources to be disseminated to users based on their present interest or work. The tools available for current awareness on the Internet are tables of contents of journals and document delivery agencies. The content pages of the journals by e-mail are mostly free of cost. SDI service can be organized by a library either by having its own computer system or available on rental basis. Research and development activities have been revolutionized through the process of document reproduction. The reprographic and micrographic technologies includes photocopying, micro copying, duplicating and printing. It has a great impact on the document delivery system.

6.4.10 Communication Technology

Communication technology is developing at a rapid pace. The need to communicate more quickly and more efficiently has become a central focus in our technological society. The major developments in this area are :-

(i) On-Line Search : Online search can help in getting immediate results with updated information of literature search. It can be used as a source of updated and nascent information supplementing the manual and CD-ROM search services. It saves time and helps the user to identify the document useful to him on the basis of information got from the search output.

(ii) Online - Technology : With the advent of the telecommunication networks came search services, often referred to as online vendors, that provide access to the databases of numerous publishers. The direct impact of computer networks is the production of large number of online databases like Chemical Abstracts Service, Biological Abstract, Food Science and Technology Abstract, Medical Literature Analysis and Retrieval Service (MEDLARS) etc. have a global coverage of chemical, medical, engineering, agriculture, aerospace and technical literature with millions of entries stored.

(iii) Electronic Mail : Electronic Mail (E-mail) is an alternative to conventional postal mail service with addition of storing and processing of messages converted into electrical signal for transmission. In libraries abstract and indexes of titles are available direct from electronic databases through e-mail.

(iv) Voice-Mail : This is the most sophisticated type of the E-mail. In a voice mail system, the computer records the message, stores and then delivers the message by using a standard telephone receiver.

(v) Teletex : Teletex is a high speed E-mail service designed to be compatible in exchange of information which allows transfer of text on memory-to-memory basis between communicating word processors.

(vi) Teletext : Teletext is a one way communication of text and graphics which makes use of computers. At present teletext services carrying current awareness type of information-news, sports, travel information, weather etc. have high priority.

(vii) Electronic Document Delivery Systems : One of the important functions of an information system is to provide material requested by its users. When the required material is not available in-house, the system may try to obtain the same from other information centre or document supply centres. An electronic document delivery system can provide immediate access to the information to the user, provided that the system is connected to the Document Supply Centre and the required information is stored in electronic media, magnetic, tape, video-disc and CD-ROM etc can effectively be used as electronic document delivery systems. This eliminates the delays in the supply of documents by conventional means.

(viii) Internet Services : Internet is a network of thousands of networks providing its users access to the world information in various fields. It is a worldwide web of interconnected university, business, military and science networks and is made up of Local Area Networks (LAN's) Metropolitan Area Networks (MAN's) and huge Wide Area Network (WAN's) connecting computers for organisation in the world. These networks are hooked together with regular dial up phone lines. Anyone willing to become its member can access information from documents, archives, pictures, sound and databases and is a helpful source especially for people engaged in research and development activity, scientists, information disseminators like libraries and information scientists, information disseminators like libraries and information scientists, people in politics, journalists etc. The internet connecting nearly 50,000 networks in about 80 countries can be accessed by 20 million people around the world for various Internet Services, Bulletin Board Service etc.

Besides this the other developments, in communication are audio-technology, audio-visual technology, video-text, fax, satellite technology, teleconference and cellular telephones.

6.5 ADVANTAGES OF INFORMATION TECHNOLOGY

Scientific and Technical libraries are changing today from simple to complex organizations. Application of modern information technologies have profound influence on the usage and reference pattern in libraries resulting in new type of demands and services. A variety of advantages can be derived by the appropriate use of IT. IT advantages can refer to anything useful data produced with the assistance of technology which allows to complete more tasks with greater accuracy and better quality in less time for lower costs. It could be higher productivity, better image of the library, improved response time or improving staff morale and motivation. In certain nature of jobs, hours of manual work are completed within minutes through IT. Perhaps, there may not be any area of operation or service where one cannot apply IT and get benefits in the following ways :-

(i) IT helps to avoid duplication of effort and work in library operations.

(ii) IT facilitates cooperation and resources sharing through library networks.

(iii) IT helps to introduce new services and improve existing services.

(iv) IT allows integration of various library operations.

(v) IT facilities faster information communication.

(vi) IT helps to increase efficiency and effectiveness of library operations.

(vii) IT helps to increase morale and motivation of library staff.

(viii) IT facilitates easy and wider access to all kinds of information sources.

(ix) IT improves productivity and image of the library.

(x) The user's have been benefited by the computerized CAS, SDI, transmission and translation services.

(xi) Through reprographic technique not only hard copies can be obtained on paper but on other media as well as microfilms and discs.

(xii) The electronic publishing and telecommunication helps to make access to world's information sources.

Information technology ultimately helps to save time, space, energy and resources.

6.6 DISADVANTAGES OF INFORMATION TECHNOLOGY

The following are disadvantages of IT :-

(i) Latest technologies required for automation is expensive.

(ii) It requires trained staff to handle the new systems, for this purpose staff training and user's training is required.

(iii) Maintainenance cost of library is increased.

(iv) It leads to unemployment because all the work will be provided with less human hands.

CONCLUSION

The role of IT in collection, storage and dissemination of information is widely recognized all over the world. Thus, we can see that Information Technology has an impact on every facet of house-keeping operations of Research and Technical libraries. It shows its impact on the time, accuracy, efficiency and effectiveness of each library operation and due to advantages of IT devices, it has become inevitable to adopt such technologies by the library professionals.

7

The Internet and Emerging Research and Technical Libaries Scenario

7.1 INTRODUCTION

The explosion of information technologies, has affected all aspects of human life including library. Huge amount of information is being generated every moment through various applications of information technologies in various media. The present day is characterized by reducing distances, shortening of time zone and digitzed storing of information. Web access has become essential in mediating a digital world. The Internet offers unparalled reaches to scientists and researchers to trace new discoveries faster than ever before. Advances in computer technology have brought most of the people as close as a mouse-click to the wealth of information. It is no longer necessary to go through volume to volume of a printed encyclopedia to access information. The information is no longer confined to books and documents in the custody of individuals or educational institutions. In the present time computer based facilities like CD's, DVD's the E-mail and Internet are available in the libraries.

7.2 INTERNET - DEFINITION

The Internet is one of the most important and complex innovations of mankind. Internet is the worlds largest network of computers that is a global network of computer networks. It is popularly known as 'The NET'. This is also known as Information Superhighway, Cyberspace, a World Wide Channel of Communication, a large store of Information, an abstract backbone of a universal network to which individual computers or networks could plug in a cyber world.

It is little difficult to define Internet comprehensively. Any attempt in this direction will be like that of blind men defining the elephant. Perhaps, it can be comprehended best by stating that it is a network of thousands of networks linked together, forming a worldwide networks. This network makes it possible for millions of people to communicate, to share information about common interests and to work on the same documents in multi-media format. It is not owned by any single individual company, institution or country but is a combined effort of networks available on the earth. Hence we can say that Internet is a wonderful information communication tool by which we can get and send the information faster beyond our imagination.

7.3 HISTORY AND GROWTH OF INTERNET

The Internet began in 1969, during the cold war when the United States Department of Defence created the ARPANET (Advanced Research Projects Agency Networks).Until a few years ago mostly students and researchers knew of it. It has attained incredible popularity amongst the general public in a very short span of time. What began in USA in 1969 as a Defence Project has today became a common medium that connects millions of computers and people all over the world. It is considered as the biggest technological break-through in media after the printing press. ARPANET was a great success, every university in USA wanted to become a part of ARPANET. In 1969, the beginning of the INTERNET consisted of four high speed networked computers located in three universities and a research institute in America. By 1970's there were 23 nodes of ARPANET . During 1980's TCP/IP protocol was established for ARPANET. This protocol became standard on 1st January 1983. It is used for transferring data back and forth and the name "INTERNET" was first used. ARPANET grew considerably during the early eighties and became the main backbone of the Internet based around the TCP/IP Protocol.

During 1990's HTML (Hypertext Markup Language) was created.HTML, is the language source code used for current Web pages. The purpose of HTML is to make pages more graphical than plain documents.. The World Wide Web (WWW) was created, and this was a huge network of web pages all around the world gathered into one web. By July 1998, over 36,000,000 computers distributed throughout the country across the globe were connected to Internet.

7.4 PRESENT AND FUTURE OF INTERNET

The growth of Internet has been global and continuous. It is growing at a rapid pace. Every magazine, newspaper, Indian and foreign is dedicating a couple of pages to it. In its short life, Internet has become an agent of revolutionary change and is one of the faster tools to facilitate democratic access to information and knowledge. It has emerged as today's greatest instruments of progress and has gradually became a part of the vital infrastructure of global social, scientific, economic, cultural and political life. Over the past decade, the use of e-mail and the web and blogs have become part of the daily routine of more than a billion Internet users. The number of Internet users is also growing tremendously. It almost doubles after every two years.

The scope of Internet is also widening as it is being used for publishing of ideas apart from being an effective tool for storage and retrieval of Information. Internet offers a variety of services used to create, browse, access, search, view and communicate information on a diverse set of topics ranging from the results of scientific experiments to discussions of recreation activities. The sources of information available on the Internet are electronic journals, technical reports, preprints, library catalogues, e-mail based information service, scientific data sets, patents, standard's, directories, reference sources, content pages of journals, database, online educational materials, usenet news etc. All these sources provide a great wealth of information which can be utilized by the Research and Technical libraries in providing information to users.

High-speed networks makes it possible for research and technical professionals to work in ways never before possible. Today, Virtual Collaborative Clinics connects medical facilities allowing doctors to manipulate high-resolution, 3-D images of MRI scans and other medical imaging. Not only can doctors consult and diagnose, but also gives surgeons an opportunity to practice before even entering the operating room, reducing the time required for actual procedure. Using this kind of virtual technology, local hospital can access resources and skills only available at larger institutions. The technology may soon be used to provide remote health care to astronauts on extended space journeys.

Now–a-days Internet has become a part of Research and Technical library environment. Internet is playing an important role in transforming the library resources and services. With the help of web based library services in the developed countries users are attending it round the clock. Internet provides links to various library sites, specializing in almost every topic and they can be directly accessed from any part of the world.

7.5 NEED OF RESEARCH AND TECHNICAL LIBRARIES TO ACCESS THE INTERNET

The need for interneting the research and technical libraries arises because in this information age the Research and Technical libraries are meeting the challenges of ever-increasing volume of information, decreasing abilities of libraries for comprehensive acquisition of documents, growing demands of increasing number of users and the complex and multifaceted user requirements. The Internet provides a more systematic solution for most of the problems of research and technical libraries. Following are the reasons for interneting the R&T libraries:-

(i) Information Explosion

In the age of Science and Technology, information explosion is the biggest problem and the effective research cannot be done without current and appropriate information. Now, we can solve this problem through the use of Internet services like FTP, WWW, E-Mail, Usenet etc.

(ii) Availability of Electronic Products and Services

A vast number of electronic information products and services such as electronic-journals, electronic-books, electronic discussion forums, technical reports, content pages of journals, library catalogues, directories and online educational material etc, are appearing at a rapidly increasing rate and are available on the Internet. The users of R&T libraries find these products attractive and use them more heavily than print sources. The research and technical libraries can avail this opportunity by using these resources.

(iii) Resource Sharing

The advent of Internet has been a boost in resource sharing. The R&T libraries which have collection of CD-ROM, magnetic disk based text, graphics, video and voice based multimedia as information in addition to the printed media have realized the usefulness of Internet in resource sharing. In India more than 1000 research and educational institutions are daily exchanging their data.

(iv) Huge Volume of Collection of Print Media

The Research and Technical libraries have huge volume of collection of print media which has made it impossible practically to locate the desired information manually. Moreover, the existing manual services have surprisingly high costs. These high costs can be reached by the use of Internet services like E-mail to another libraries etc.

(v) Users Need

The main goal of the R&T library is to provide latest information to the users and this is possible only by using electronic information services. Full text documents and information is also available via internet E-mail can be used for delivering information to the users. The speed of delivery, the ability to monitor information in a compatible form are the keys to effectively meet the users needs.

(vi) Access to Unlimited Sources of Information:-

The Internet provides access to unlimited sources of information which are not conveniently obtainable through other means. Since we are in the age of electronic communication, researchers can carry forward their work on the internet in ways that are similar to the traditional ways.

Thus, Internet is the cheapest and fastest means to get information, provide information and compile information

7.6 APPLICATION OF INTERNET IN RESEARCH AND TECHNICAL LIBRARIES SERVICES

Internet has become an essential and indispensable tool for information professionals, researchers, doctors, engineers, agriculturists etc. The Internet has the tremendous impact on Research and Technical libraries information services. The Internet has increased the scope of all services. Some of the major library services that can be offered through Internet are as follows:-

(i) Acquisition of Documents

Internet has made simple and speedy purchase of information sources/documents like books, journals and electronic publications. Publishers catalogues, reviews, directories, price lists are available on the internet. Orders and recommendations can be set online.

(ii) Classification and Cataloguing

Preparing standard catalogue without much effort has become possible due to Internet and the WWW. Librarians can check the catalogues of other libraries like that of Library of Congress and confirm the information required for a record which can be easily ascertained from the original document. Several libraries are opting the Cyber Dewey Decimal Classification summaries on the WWW. The Cyber Dewey websites includes alphabetical index to Dewey Decimal classification.

(iii) Circulation

Internet has made the circulation of in-house documents much easier. After the technical processing, the new documents can be placed in the OPAC on the day of acquisition itself and readers with Internet connection at the University or at home or at the research institute can browse and reserve the books while sitting right at their offices or at home within seconds after arrival of the books in the library.

(iv) Reference and Information Service

Internet can be successfully utilized for providing short range and long range reference service because various primary and secondary sources of information are available online from many sites. The electronic versions of reference books are available for reference directly from the websites for their publishers or from libraries that have them in their electronic storage systems and have network license from publishers to permit users to access those sources online.

Various electronic reference materials available on Internet are Encyclopaedia Britannica Online, Mc - Graw Hill Encyclopaedia of Science and Technology, Eyewitness Encyclopaedia of Nature, The Grolier's Encylopaedia Online, Grolier's Mc Graw-Hill Encyclopaedia of Mammalian Biology, Eyewitness Encylopaedia of Space and Universe, the Way Things Work etc. The librarians can use these databases and sources to respond to queries from the users.

(v) Communication

There are various 'communication tools available on "Net". It includes direct communication (e-mail, chat etc), online conferencing, distributed information resources, file transfer and many other valuable tools and resources are available to access and collect information on Internet. The most important means of communication on the Internet is E-mail. The main attraction of E-mail lies in its speed, it is much more powerful than paper-mail. E-mail is a network, service that enable users to send and receive messages and data. With the E-mail we can send and receive anything we use or create that is words, documents, programs, photos, images, sounds, messages and data. It is one of the most popular services of Internet. It is the latest, most economical and highly used modes of communication. Libraries can use E-mail facility extensively to communicate with the publishers, book-sellers and vendors of the other library products and services with scholars, librarians and users across the globe.

Bulletin Board Service (BBS) is a forum for users to browse and exchange information. BBS usually comprises of small group of users who have a common interest. Usenet is a system of distributed bulletin board looking after discussion groups or chat lines who regularly gather to speak, to exchange views and comments. Usenet is a world wide community of exchange views and comments. It is a world wide community of electronic bulletin board services developed to facilitate discussion groups called Newsgroups, in which any user of Internet can participate in a public dialogue with every one else on the networks.

World Wide Web also known as Web, WWW, W3 is the most powerful navigation tool on the Internet. It enables a person to move freely from one website to another. WWW is a system, based on hypertext for providing, organizing and accessing a wide variety of resources (text, images/graphics and sound) that are available on Internet. It is an advanced browsing service. It allows linking together information stored in different computers. File Transfer Protocol (FTP) is used to transfer files from one host computer to another.

(vi) Electronic Publishing

Internet facilitates the publishing of reports, summaries of research or conferences. It has brought electronic publishing within the reach of anyone with an Internet access account.

(vii) Information Generation

A variety of information can be generated on WWW by libraries such as on-line public access catalogues, notices and call for research paper and library information on the home papers.

In short, any kind of information available anywhere in the world is available on one's own personal computer at an affordable cost.

(viii) Resource Sharing

With the advent of Internet major libraries are now available online through Internet and hence directly accessible from any part of the world. Librarians can have access to the catalogue of various libraries attached to the universities and research and technical institutions in the world and accordingly place a request for their users.

(ix) Websites

Now Research and Technical libraries can create their websites and through these websites they can inform about various services, products, events and courses offered by them.

(x) Current Awareness Service :-

The tools available for current awareness on Internet are tables of contents of journals discussion forums and unsent news.

7.7 SOURCES OF INFORMATION AVAILABLE ON INTERNET

Following are the various sources of Information available on Internet :-

(i) Scientific and Engineering Network News, a fee based monthly guide to internet resources for scientists and engineers. (*http://www.senn.com/*)

(ii) History of Science, Technology and Medicine, is an excellent biographical dictionary, documents on every area of technology, a directory of scientific institutions and electronic journals.

(*http://www.ascap.unimelb.edu.au/hstm/hstm_ove.htm*).

(iii) NASA Homepage, is the homepage for the National Aeronautics and Space Administration. While clicking on "Gallery" one can see photographs taken from space. (*http://www* fsfc. nasa. gov/ NASA_homepage. html).

(iv) Planet Science, site contains selected news and feature stories of selected topics from the pages of world famous science weekly 'News Scientists' (*www.newscientist.com*)

(v) Science Daily, site provides latest science research news (*www.sciencedaily.com*).

(vi) Volcano World brings modern and near real time volcano information to the Internet using remote sensing images and other data collections. (*http:// volcano*. und >nodak.edu/ vw.html).

(vii) Dictionary of Science and Biotechnology (http:// biotech. chem.. indiana. ed/ pages/ dictionary/ html.)

(viii) Mc-Graw-Hill Encyclopaedia of Science and Technology. (*http://www.mhreference,com/EST/est.htm*)

(ix) Encylopaedia Britannica Online, the worlds oldest, most authoritative and famous Encyclopaedia is available in 30 volumes. (*http://www.eb.com*).

(x) National Air and Space Museum has a largest and unique collection of document on all media about everything.(www. Nasm.si.edu)

(xi) Animal Veterinary Medical Association, site is an excellent source for caring for our pet. (www.avma. org).

(xii) Tree Doctor, site helps to find out about tree diseases and pests, tree topping etc. (*www.1* stresource. com/ t/ treedoc/ .)

(xiii) CDC Home Page, gives information on diseases,

health risks, prevention and guidelines. (*http://www.cdc.gov*)

(xiv) TIPTOP, the Internet pilot to Physics (*http://www.tp.umu.se/TIPTOP/*);

(xv) Chemistry Center of the American Chemical Society (http:/www.Chem Center.org/).

(xvi) WWW Virtual Library-Engineering (*http://arioch.gsfc.nasa-gov/wwwv. engineering.html*);

(xvii) Mathematics on the Internet (*http://w-math.ams.org/*).

(xviii) WWW Virtual library –Medicine (*http://www.* ohsu. educ/ cliniweb wwvl/);

(xix) Biology-National Biological Information Infrastructure (*http://www.nbs.gov/nbii/*)

Some other popular search engines are :-

(i) **Yahoo:** Yahoo is a compreshensive directory of over 80,000 Internet resources. It provides comprehensive online products and services to consumers and businesses worldwide. (*http://www.yahoo.com*).

(ii) **Alta Vista:** Featuring web and newsgroups search engine as well as paid submission services. Indexes over 30 million web pages. (http:// altavista. digital.com).

(iii) **Lycos** : Lycos is a largely automated index, just like altavista. It is one of the earliest web search systems. (*http://www.lycos.com*).

(iv) **Hotbot** : It indexes web pages as well as multimedia, audio, FTP, PDF and MS-Word files from around the world. (*http://www.hotbot.com*).

(v) **Northern light:** The Northern light searches and also automatically categorize the pages they find displaying a listing of folders from integrated web and article searching. (*http://www.Northernlight.com*).

(vi) **Infoseek** : Infoseek is an index similar to Altavista.

Some keywords are given to find relevant pages and finds the first 10 web websites that match the words (*http://www* infoseek.com)

(vii) **Excite:-** Excite is an index like Altavista with a concept search which is supposed to find relevant pages even if we don't type exactly the same words the pages used. Excite also has sections with reviews of web pages, city directories, white pages and many more. (*http://www* excite.com)

(viii) **Web crawler :** Web crawler is an automated indexer that crawls around the web cataloguing indexing of every page it comes across. It offers minimal context for each page it returns that is just, the name of the page and a link to it, without the contents of the page. (*http://www* webcrawler.com).

CONCLUSION

Internet has helped to remove barriers of distance and time. The modern technology is applied in speedy retrieval of information most consistently. Information technology with Biotechnology and Bioinformatics provides greater avenues for easy access to information, improving efficiency of functioning of libraries education system and ultimately to improve the quality of life. For researchers, Internet is the library of the present and future. A growing number of users are using the Internet for research for searching information concerned with their research field based on latest facts. Thus, the use of Internet in R&T libraries has brought efficiency in services ranging from acquisition of documents to the retrieval of information as well as creation of knowledge.

8

Planning Research And Technical Libraries Buildings

8.1 INTRODUCTION

Le Carbusier, has rightly said, "the plan is the generator of architecture". If the book is soul of the library, library building is the body in which the soul dwells. Hence it is highly essential to examine all factors before constructing a building for a library. Planning is one of the most important tasks for the most efficient use of whatever space may be allotted for library purposes. The idea and the knowledge of planning a new library building has come to stay as one of the important responsibilities of modern librarianship so that the library managers may not face the problem of accommodation. A poorly planned building can seriously handicap users and staff; while a good one can very efficiently contribute to the intellectual health of the institution as a whole. Planning a library building should reflect ideas to make it both an efficient functional unit of the parent organization as well as aesthetically designed place conducive to study and research.

The main activities of a library are to collect and process library materials, to store and display them, and finally to disseminate the information contained in these materials. Therefore sufficient and separate accommodation should be provided for the activities ranging from clerical, bibliographical, informational to administrative nature of work. In planning the library building all these factors have to be kept in view.

8.2 BASIC PREREQUISITES AND CONSIDERATIONS FOR PLANNING A RESEARCH AND TECHNICAL LIBRARY BUILDING

Following are the basic prerequisites and considerations for planning a R&T library building :-

8.2.1 Site Selection/Location:

In planning a research and technical library the first important step is the selection of the site for the library. The library should be located in an area which is most accessible to its users. A R&T library being functional unit, should be located either in the main building housing the organization or in a separate building easily accessible and in close proximity to it. It should be convenient for laboratory and divisions of the institution whom the library serves. Soil should be tested and it should be termite free. In case a library is related to research laboratory, then it should not be located in the area near inflammatory material like petrol and gases. Library building should have asthetic surrounding with vertical and horizontal expansion of building must be possible.

8.2.2 Design of Research And Technical Library Building

For designing a functional and decorative library building for the convenience of those who will use it, it is essential to consult an architecture. In designing such a library the points that are generally kept in view are :-

(i) The design of library building should be simple and functional,

(ii) It should be convenient to the users,

(iii) Construction of library building is a costly affair. Therefore cost-analysis of library building should be undertaken and cost of per square feet of construction should be calculated.

(iv) Flexibility and adaptability for future changes in library service should be taken into consideration. Reshuffling and reorganization of various section of the library should be possible.

(v) An adequate parking space should be there for those who make use of the library.

(vi) Allocation of space to different sections should be provided in such a way that normal functioning in the library is not subjected to any hindrance.

(vii) Library building should be designed for 'open access system'.

(viii) Fixed construction implies constructing separate room for separate work. On the other hand in modular construction no room is constructed, besides a few rooms for administration, technical work, physical facilities etc, the space inside is left open in the form of hall/halls. In these halls work area can be created by erecting temporary partitions made of wood, ply, racks, or even bricks. In modular system pillars are established first, then the roofs are build and lastly the walls are established. Planning of a library building is so that it consists of a number of modules, having no permanent internal walls dividing the floor are into rooms. Each floor is supported by pillars at regular intervals and these pillars are often partly hollow to accommodate plumbing, electric wiring and air conditioning ducts. Except for core service areas such as staircases, which are enclosed by permanent walls, the whole of the floor area can be subdivided into rooms and departments by placing free-standing book cases, partitions and furniture where desired. This type of modular construction ensures flexibility and through modular system cost-analysis of library building can be undertaken in advance. Reorganization and reshuffling is also possible through modular system and moreover modular system requires less supervision.

8.2.3 Internal Organization

Library building should be constructed keeping in view the requirements for the next twenty years. Internal organization of R&T libraries should be based on the functional requirements of different sections, so allocation of space to different sections is the important constituent of R&T library building. Librarian must allocate space to different sections keeping in view the total specified square feet area for the construction of library. Permanent type of fixed walls should be avoided to need any future unknown requirement.

8.3 ALLOCATION OF SPACE

Planning of space is an important task for its optimum utilization. Allocation of space to different sections of Research & Technical Libraries for its effective functioning is as follows:-

8.3.1 Entrance and Exhibit Area

Entrance of research and technical library should be near the main pedestrian traffic so that users may not have to walk long distance to have access to the library. Exhibitions and book displays are organized in the R&T libraries to make the people aware of latest arrivals in the library so that is why exhibitions are to be organized at such a place were the users mostly pass that is it should be near the entrance of the library.

8.3.2 Reading Room

One or two reading rooms are kept in a R&T library. Some libraries keep one reading room for book-material and one for non-book material such as film-strips, microfilms, micro cards etc. The area of reading room depends upon total number of users to be enrolled in future. Space provided for each user is 3.3 sq. ft. About reading area and stack area one of the following arrangements may be followed:-

(i) **Central Location :** In this arrangement stack area is surrounded by the reading area that is stack area is in the centre.

(ii) **Peripheral Location :** In this arrangement reading area is surrounded by stack area that is reading area is in the centre.

(iii) **Vertical Location :** In this arrangement reading area and stack area are adjacent to each other that is both remain side by side.

(iv) **Rear Location :** In this arrangement reading area and stack area are separated from each other.

The most suitable area for reading room is near the main stack room so that users may not face any inconvenience while studying or reading in the reading room. The reading-room and stack-room should have the benefit of natural ventilation. Each window in a reading room should be so placed that there is sufficient natural light on the reading table. However, artificial light through electricity is also essential. Arrangements should be made to ensure that every reader gets sufficient light. Special tables, fitted with tube lights may be made. In the library such bulbs and tubes should be used that do not strain on eyes.

8.3.3 Technical Section

The total area for technical services depend upon a number of books and documents to be added yearly, total number of staff to be recruited, levels of technical work to be performed. On an average each technical staff member is to be provided with 10 sq. ft. of space. The space for technical section should be sufficient so that the books received in the acquisition centre may be shifted to the technical section. There should be combined acquisition cum technical section hall so that processing of documents should be undertaken immediately.

8.3.4 Mechanical Area

Area for mechanical operations depends upon the number of mechanical devices which the library is going to procure. The mechanical devices include reprographic equipment, lifts, microform, readers, computers etc. A separate room is desirable with adequate control of lighting, ventilation, room temperature etc.

8.3.5 Area for Services

Area for services in a R&T libraries depends upon the type of services to be provided by the librarian. R&T libraries mostly organize documentation services, bibliographic services and reference service. The area of such a type of services depends upon following factors :-

(i) The volume of work required for organizing such services.

(ii) Overall space of the library.

(iii) Staff Strength.

(iv) Number of users for whom services are to be provided.

Within the service area should be located, the circulation or charging desk, the card catalogue, atlas and dictionary stands, file cabinets etc. and reference collection.

8.3.6 Stack Area or Room

Stack room should be near the reading hall. The area for stack room depends upon the pattern of stacking to be followed. The most common and traditional method of stacking is the construction of double sided stacks with the height of 7 to 8ft. The stack room should be placed centrally so that it is easily accessible from every part of the library. It should be placed so as to run from east to west, the primary reason being avoidance of direct sun. The area of stack room depends upon following factors :-

(i) Type of sources to be stored in the stack room.

(ii) Annual growth rate of collection for next 20 years.

(iii) Weeding policy.

(iv) Overall organizational structure of the organsiation whom the library serves.

8.3.7 Area for Administration Work

Area for administrative work depends upon space requirement of the librarian and number of staff in the library so that duties may be performed without any disturbance. The area of administrative function is located at a distant place were users normally do not pass or visit.

Following are the other factors which should be kept in mind while planning a library building :-

(i) Design of library building should be asthetic and simple. Too much of architectural designs should be avoided. It should be capable of horizontal and vertical expansion.

(ii) The structure of the library building should be rectangular. It should not be hexagonal or circular in dimension. As it is easier to expand the rectangular building as has as horizontal expansion is concerned. Moreover traditional type of equipment/furniture may be used in rectangular structure building where as for a circular building special type of equipment is needed.

(iii) For sound players or video-players type of material, reading rooms should be sound proof and all types of acoustic effects should be clearly studied and any effect like echo, unreasonable sound disturbance should be avoided.

(iv) To avoid any voice due to foot steps, librarian must plan to use poly-vinyl tiles in reading room or any other area which is visited most by the users.

(v) Any possibility to electric problem like short circuiting or fire should be considered before hand.

(vi) Cooperation of librarian, engineer and architecture is essential. Engineer provides technical know how regarding quality, cost and material aspect of building. Architect is supposed to advice and make a plan for exterior and interior outlook for planning and cost of building. Librarian is concerned with the functional and operational aspects of building.

8.4 STANDARDS FOR LIBRARY BUILDING

To provide compatibility and uniformity regarding the construction of library building, various standards have been established. The Indian standard IS: 1553-1960 Code of Practice relating to primary elements in the design of library building gives information.

Besides this, survey of existing R&T library buildings and their operational and functional problems, opinions of functional staff working in various libraries, average size of different types of libraries in terms of the average number of books, bound volumes of periodicals, number of current periodicals for display, the number of seats for readers, strength of staff, different kinds of rooms required for different libraries are very useful in planning R&T library building.

CONCLUSION

The effective allocation of space for R&T library is one of the most important initial tasks to be performed in planning a library service. In fact it is likely to be a continuous activity as changes must be made to accommodate the growth of the collection and development of various functions. Every possible source of assistance should be exploited in designing even the most modest libraries. Among these are publications dealing with the subject, manufacturers literature and most rewarding of all, functioning libraries. Time and effort spent at the stage of planning of R&T libraries will at least minimize the chance of avoidable errors.

9

Planning and Acquistion of Research and Technical Libaries Equipment

9.1 INTRODUCTION

While a good collection and effective services are hallmarks of a good R&T library or Information centres, a well-planned building with well-designed furniture and fittings are equally important for efficient operation of a library service. It has been said that a library building is incomplete without proper furniture, fittings and furnishings, library equipment should be functional, strong, easy to keep clean and easily repaired. It should be able to withstand external agents such as humidity, rapid changes of temperature, insects, pests and fungus.

9.2 FACTORS RESPONSIBLE FOR DECIDING THE TYPE AND QUALITY OF LIBRARY EQUIPMENT

A large number of companies undertake production of various equipment. They advertise their equipment through trade literature and trade catalogues. Due to the availability of large varieties of equipment, there is a need to spend economically and for this purpose a proper decision is required regarding the purchasing of library equipment. For this purpose a committee may be appointed to decide the type and quality of equipment and before deciding the type and quality of library equipment the committee must be aware of the following factors :-

(i) Availability of total funds for equipment,

(ii) The number and type of equipment library is to purchase.

(iii) Availability of floor area in square feet.

The committee may consult trade catalogues and may also visit the commercial organizations and shops. The committee members should prefer to visit the exhibitions were not only the exhibitions are displayed but demonstrator is also provided. The committee should also consider the maintenance cost as it is not possible for large number of libraries to bear maintenance cost. Cost of servicing should also be considered. The servicing facilities should be locally available. Some equipment may require special type of material which may not be available locally so this point must also be kept in mind.

The above mentioned factors would influence the choice and design of library furniture as well as the material to be used for the furniture. The material used may be softwood, hardwood, metal, plastic etc.

9.3 NEED FOR FURNITURE/EQUIPMENT

The furniture and equipment are needed due to following reasons :-

(i) To store or stack the documents,

(ii) To preserve the collection for longer duration and posterity;

(iii) To read the micro-media as it cannot be read with the naked eye.

(iv) A variety of Information Technology equipment such as computers, printers, micro-film readers, fax machines etc. are needed.

(v) Furniture is needed for use of the staff and readers.

9.4 SELECTION OF LIBRARY FURNITURE/ EQUIPMENT

The team required for selecting library furniture/ equipment should include the librarian, the architect, the administrator and consultant if and when necessary. The librarian should choose the shelving, catalogues and technical equipment and the architect should choose chairs and tables because these are the wares with which he is concerned throughout his professional life. The equipment to be procured by the R&T libraries should be asthetic in look and convenient in operation. The acquisition of equipment and collection depends upon the type of institution with which the library is concerned. If the library is to develop micro-forming collection then it will procure micro-film or microfiche reader, printer and the cabinets accordingly.

9.5 CRITERIA FOR SELECTION OF VARIOUS KINDS OF FURNITURE AND EQUIPMENT

The essential items of equipment required by R&T libraries are as under :-

9.5.1 Shelving

Shelving is specifically designed to hold books. Standard size shelving is to be designed for R&T library. It may be of either wood or steel. It is recommended that steel furniture should be preferred as it has greater capacity and is easier to maintain and manipulate. It is advisable to have all the shelving units of the same height giving complete flexibility in re-arranging the layout of the library. Shelving sizes most suitable for R&T libraries are :-

Height 6 feet 10 inches (82 inches) giving six shelves. 7 feet 6 inches (90 inches) giving seven shelves, (The height of the ceiling would affect the choice of shelving height) on which 126 books or 110 volumes of bound periodicals can be accommodated.

Width 3 feet (36 inches) from centre to centre. (longer shelves are not advisable).

If the shelving is to stand against walls, single faced shelving is required, otherwise double faced shelving can be used. A stock of 10,000 books, 80,000 bound journals and a couple of thousand reports, with 30 feet range of double-faced shelves will require a floor space of about 12,00 sq.ft.

A good appearance, durability and sufficient strength to support the weight load is essential. Shelving should be adjustable to take books of different heights.

9.5.2 Tables and Chairs for Readers

Tables and chairs are required for clientele. The number and size of the tables will be determined by the space allotted for readers. The furniture should be of wood or metal. Wood has an advantage of being more attracted and warm in appearance. Table tops should not have highly polished surfaces; besides reflecting light into the reader's eyes, a polished surface scrapes easily and takes on stains,. The height of the table should be 30 inches from the floor. A table should be of 36×60 inches and should serve four readers. For convenience of readers and proper arrangement, a distance of 3½inch is left between rows. The distance between the wall and the last row of tables should be five feet. Chairs should be comfortable that would support for both reading and writing and should be reasonably light in weight but not too light to be knocked down easily. The seat of the chair should be 18 inches from the floor. Some chairs, particularly in the area where current periodicals are shelved, will entice readers. A few stools in some places, perhaps near the card catalogue cabinets or a bench with padded top as a convenient seat are sometimes of worth consideration.

Every staff member with special task, to perform should have his own desk and chair of a type that suits his duties. The head of the service may require a large, executive style desk to accommodate the major projects pertinent to his position. Some desks should accommodate typewriters and computers. An extra work table may be needed in some offices.

9.5.3 Study Carrels

Some individual seating either as carrels or small tables where the readers could leave his research documents for several days offer privacy and give opportunities for continued work. Very often they are located near the reference collection or the bound volumes collection which are extensively used by researchers.

9.5.4 Circulation or Charging Desk

This is the key functional area of the library and normally the counter is placed at the main entrance, and adequate space is kept for easy entry and exit. It is so designed, that the most important activities, issue and return of books is conducted smoothly and without any hindrance. The size of the counter depends on the number of readers to be served at one time Adequate space should be provided in the counter to shelve books returned and to store all essential records, including the charging trays. A property counter or a pigeon hole rack is generally placed near the issue counter, where the visitors or readers can leave their personal belongings before going inside the library. Provision is made near the counter for notice boards, display of latest book jackets or other exhibits.

9.5.5 Public Catalogue Cabinets

Public Catalogue is the key to the document collection in a library and is frequently used by the readers as well as the library staff. This should also be placed near the entrance and not far from the counter. Sufficient space should be left near the catalogue cabinets to make consultation easier. The catalogue cabinets are generally made up of wood. A few high stools may be placed near the catalogue cabinet, to make lengthy consultation comfortable. Provision is also made in the catalogue cabinet for small drawout writing board where the readers can note down the contents of the catalogue cards.

9.6 OTHER EQUIPMENT REQUIRED FOR R&T LIBRARIES ARE AS UNDER

Microforms of several types now in use require equipment or cabinets designed especially for each kind. Steel glass almirahas are suitable for storing electronic media, like magnetic discs, microfilms, microfiches etc. Short strips of microfilm may be kept into pockets and filed in drawers. Microfiche in large quantity can be filed in cabinets. Boxes are more suitable for archival records and cabinet drawers for maps and drawing.

Besides, this other furniture and equipment required for R&T libraries is microform reading machines, duplicating machines, vertical file for pamphlets, trade catalogues, charging trays, book trolleys, cupboards, wardrobes, lockers, catalogue card box, reading-room tables, reading-room chair, side rack, seminar room furniture i.e. table and chair, notice boards, black-board, charging counter, typewriters, filing cabinets, steel almirahas, scanner, slide projector, overhead projector, name and sign plates, newspaper stands, pamphlet boxes, paper trimmer, periodical racks, vertical card filing units, waste paper baskets etc.

CONCLUSION

Just as a library building is a specialized structure with specific functions, the furniture for a library has to be custom designed for each function. The needs of furniture and equipment of individual departments and sections should be given careful consideration so that the users and the staff experience, ease, comfort, convenience and efficiency in their work. Generally library furniture is of two types, wooden and metal. Now-a-days plastic furniture is also increasingly in evidence. It is advisable to visit some libraries equipped with standard and elegant furniture and fittings before taking a decision.

10

Personnel Management in Research and Technical Libraries

10.1 INTRODUCTION

A well-equipped and well - managed library is a foundation of modern education structure. All the library activities, functions, and operations are carried out by people, whether these are manual or in electronic system. Behind all the primary, designing organisation, implementation and performance there is a human mind. A library for its effective functioning requires several types of resources but the human resource is at the zenith of all other resources.

Employees constitute the most valuable resource of a R&T library. Effective functioning of a library depends upon sound personnel management. The human element has always been a key factor in resource moblisation. Staff is the key to effective functioning of a R&T library as the image of any service institution greatly depends on the caliber and efforts of its staff members. Howsoever, excellent collection a library may have, it becomes meaningless in the absence of well trained and competent library staff. It is considered as the most important component that can bring together the documents and its users in a meaningful way. Those who administer the services in a scientific-technical library must be well suited to the work. Good service should be efficient and flexible, rendered in a dignified and pleasant manner.

10.2 DEFINITION OF PERSONNEL MANAGEMENT

The management of human resources more widely known as "Personnel Management" is one of the most important aspects of Management of an organization. Personnel management refers to that aspect of management process which is concerned with increasing effectiveness of human performance in an organization. Personal management is a generic term which is concerned with the process of getting the best out of the employees of an organization by means of judicious selection, tactful dealing and by seeking their replacement whenever necessary. The management of manpower resources is the basic function of personnel management. The aim of Personnel Management is to utilize the optimum use of personnel power of workers and to get cooperation from one and all. It is an approach, an established system, a technique and a philosophy of management.

For proper personnel management, a dynamic organization is essential. Healthy working conditions for the workers, and maximum output without wastage of energies are to be ensure. Individual and human elements are taken into consideration while laying down conditions of work.

Personnel management is concerned with two components that is 'personnel' which means people and 'management' which means responsibility for accomplishment.

The British Institute of Personnel Management in the

U.K. considers personnel management as "the part of the management function which is primarily concerned with the human relationships with an organization. Its objective is the maintenance of those relationships on a basis which, by consideration of the well-being of the individual, enables all those engaged in the undertaking to make their maximum personal contribution to the effective working of the undertaking.

According to Encylopaedia of Management, "Personnel Management" is based upon a "well rounded, planned, executed and evaluated approach to employees recruitment, use and development.

The Society of Personnel Administration of America considers personnel administration as the art of acquiring, developing and maintaining the competent workplace in order to achieve and accomplish the organizational goals with maximum efficiency and economy.

On the whole, personnel management is responsible for several activities and functions and helps the management in achieving their major goals and policies. In other words, it is concerned with the basic function of management of getting better results with the collaboration of people. In this process it is mainly concerned with methods of recruitment, selection, qualifications, training and placement of the personnel and their terms of employment, promotion, working conditions, motivation and morale, salary scales, status, staff welfare etc. In fact, the primary and the most obvious aim of personnel management is to secure adequate and efficient employees to achieve the overall objective of an organization.

10.3 AIMS OF PERSONNEL MANAGEMENT IN R&T LIBRARIES

Following are the aims of personnel management :-

(i) Optimum Output

The aim of personnel management in R&T libraries is to maximize output and profit. It is achieved by securing optimum contribution from the staff employed in an institution/library.

(ii) Development of Workers Capacities

Personnel management helps the workers to develop their capacities to the maximum so that they contribute maximum to their institution. This is secured by enabling the workers to derive maximum satisfaction from their work.

(iii) Development of Team Spirit

Personnel management helps to develop team spirit. They are made to feel that they, as a group, have achieved their goal.

10.4 FUNCTIONS OF PERSONNEL MANAGEMENT IN R&T LIBRARIES

Personnel management is a staff function. It is advisory in nature. These responsibilities may take the form of the following activities :-

(i) The formulation of policy and development of plans;

(ii) Staffing, which includes, securing, selecting and placing manpower..

(iii) Controlling working conditions in order to develop and effectively utilize the service of personnel on the job;

(iv) Providing various services to employees, seeking thereby to encourage self-improvement and increased efficiency.

(v) Maintenance of personnel records and personnel research.

The personnel management in R&T libraries be grouped under the following broad headings :-

(i) Job Analysis,

(ii) Job Evaluation,

(iii) Staffing

(iv) Recruitment and Selection,

(v) Placement,

(vi) Induction and Training,

(vii) Wage and Salary Administration.

10.4.1 Job Analysis

The first and foremost function of personnel management is the job analysis. It involves the analysis of the contents of each job to be performed in an institution. The assigning of right work to the right person using management techniques is known as job analysis. The data to be obtained should be comprehensive and reliable. It should be accurate. The data should include the specific activities, responsibilities, special information needed by the employee, how the work is to be performed, working conditions and physical demands. The job data about methods may be obtained from the employees through questionnaires, interviews, discussion and observation. It can be used for the preparation of job description, for career's guidance, personnel selection, training programmes and work study. It consists of collecting, consolidating and recording various items of job information. It includes both job description and job specification.

(i) Job Description : Job analysis leads to Job Description Job description is a fundamental feature of personnel management. In case of job description an employee is given a copy of his major functions, duties and responsibilities with his contract of employment. Job description can be used for a number of purposes; for planning the overall establishments; for reviewing the organizational structure, including transfer of holders of posts from one position to another position; for job evaluation; to give employees a list of their responsibilities; to send out to applicants who reply to advertised vacancies and for staff appraisal. The contents of job description constitutes the following aspects:-

(i) Name of the position.

(ii) Pay scale, allowances and other facilities,

(iii) Qualification and Experience.

(iv) Duties and responsibilities.

(v) Promotional Avenues.

(vi) Methods of Evaluating Performance.

(vii) Retirement Benefits.

Thus, the purpose of job description is to identity a job and to provide clear description of duties.

(ii) Job Specification : This is applied to the description of the physical and mental abilities required for the job. The specific skills of the job required, the capacity to handle the job, judgment required in decision making and the experience required to carry it out are some of the special characteristics of job specification. For example – the qualification for the post of an Assistant Librarian in the computer section of a library needs a good command over the computer technology as well as its application in the management of libraries and information centres.

(iii) Personnel Specification : For specified jobs having special requirements, suitable personnel is required to handle them. In a special library the top posts are reserved for some one with an appropriate degree in the concerned subject field and adequate qualifications in library and information science.

10.4.2 Job Evaluation

Job evaluation is an essential part of effective personnel management. It meets the needs of the organisation and its personnel who wants to know how he/she is performing and what will happen as a result of the evaluation. Standard methods of job evaluation are :-

(i) Ranking method,

(ii) Classification system,

(iii) Factor comparison method,

(iv) Point system.

(i) Ranking Method : This involves comparison of one job with other in terms of technical skill, complexity, work environment and such other factors which determine the value of the job. Getting necessary data of all the jobs, they are ranked from low to high job and works fairly well when the number of jobs to be evaluated is very few. In this method, only broad qualities of the jobs are considered and not in respect of the specific factors to measure the value of the job.

(ii) Job Classification : This is traditional method of job evaluation. It is essential that professional jobs are carried out by professionals. However, in any library, there are a large number of routine and clerical jobs, which do not require professional training or capability. Such jobs must be performed by supporting staff. The classification of jobs is based on the kind of work to be performed and the responsibility involved in the work. The jobs are given on the basis of qualification, experience and common sense of the candidates. But this system is not based on scientific principles.

(iii) Factor Comparison Method : This method presupposes that the pay-scales of each job is fixed by taking a number of factors into consideration. Each factor is assigned a weightage according to its importance for the job/organization and finally the job level of the position and the monetary compensation attached to it.

(iv) Point System : In this system, relevant factors of each job are found out. Each of these factors is assigned points. These factors include skill, effort, responsibility and job conditions. Each of these factors is sub-divided into following sub-factors such as education, experience, physical demand, mental or visual demand, supervising responsibility, decision making etc. All these factors are assessed by points which in turn, indicated the rate. The salary scale of each job is fixed on the basis of points of each sub-factor such as education, experience, physical demand, mental or visual demand, supervising responsibility, decision making etc. All these factors are assessed by point which in turn, indicate the rate. The salary scale of each job is fixed on the basis of points of each sub-factor of a job.

10.4.3 Staffing

Staffing means putting a right person at the right job. This is the vital function of personnel management. Actual recruitment is preceded by job analysis, job description, job specification, class analysis, fixing the number of each kind of job, its qualifications and salary scale.

In case of Research and Technical libraries the professional library staff is under one or the other of the following titles :-

(i) Chief Librarian/Documentation/Information/Research Officer.

(ii) Deputy Librarian/Documentation/Information/Research Officer.

(iii) Assistant Librarian/Documentation/Information/Research Officer.

(iv) Documentation/Indexer/Abstractor/Bibliographic/Documentation Assistant/Technical Assistant/Professional Assistant.

The professional posts may also be given the

following titles in a library, especially where there is a functional type of organisation.

(i) Librarian.

(ii) Assistant Librarian/Accession or Acquisition Librarian/Maintenance Librarian/Senior Classifier/ Senior Cataloguer/Documentalist Assistant Reference Librarian.

Staff Formula for Professionals Working in R&T Libraries

According to **M.A. Gopinath,** the following should be the Staff Formula for professionals.

	Section & Functions	*Quantum of Work per person.*
(i)	**Book Section:**	
	Selection, ordering and accessioning of books/ documents received.	6,000 documents, annually added.
(ii)	**Periodical Section :**	
	Ordering, Receipt, preparation and display of current periodicals, their cumulation and preparing for binding.	1,500 periodicals received.
(iii)	**Technical Processing Section :**	
	Classification and Cataloguing	2000 documents annually added.
(iv)	**Circulation Section :**	
	Charging and discharging of books.	1,500 Gate hours, circulation counter is kept open.
(v)	**Reference Section**	50 Queries/readers in a day.
(vi)	**Maintenance Section**	One person for every 500 volumes to be replaced in a day and one person for every 1,00,00 volumes in the library.
(vii)	**Documentation/Information Service Section.**	1.5 Man-year on an average for each service.
(viii)	**Supervisory Staff**	One chief librarian and two heads of units.

Note : It has been suggested that professionals should be at least one-third of the whole-staff.

10.4.4 Recruitment and Selection

The recruitment of library staff is to be planned properly. The main aim of recruitment should be to secure best candidates for performing specific jobs in a library. The recruitment and selection procedures must be performed in a systematic manner. The recruitment and selection methods must be linked with the environment. High quality selection on the part of the interviews should have a full understanding of the occupational, social and organizational skills needed to fit both the job and the organisation. Therefore, the purpose of any recruitment exercise is to select the person who will carry out the job most efficiently in the circumstances of an organisation.

Once the posts are identified for recruitment, advertisement goes to the newspapers, professional newsletters, employment offices calling for applications or recommendations for the posts. Advertisements should clearly mention the basic information about name of the position, qualification and experience, pay-scales and other facilities, duties and responsibilities, essential and desirable qualifications for the post etc. After calling for the applications, selection committee is constituted for the purpose.

Important methods normally used for selecting the right candidates are :-

(i) Interview and (ii) Tests.

(i) Interview: The interview is the most common method of selection of candidates. The interview will assess the candidate's personal, relations, style, motivations, and attitudes, ability to adjust with change and meet challenge and suitability for the specific functions of the job. The process of selection at the interview stage should consider following important qualities :-

(i) Appearance and speech.
(ii) Quality of intelligence and standard of education.
(iii) Evidence of application and capacity for work.
(iv) Ability to reason and solve problems.
(v) Sociability, co-operativeness, flexibility.
(vi) Initiative and creativity, originality, self-sufficiency.
(vii) Organizational skills.
(viii) Written skills, original work, theoretical contribution.
(ix) Professionalism, integrity.

(ii) Tests : Sometimes tests are conducted for selection of good candidates to assess the intelligence, proficiency, aptitude and personality of the candidates. Intelligence test are intended to know the mental alertness, power of understanding reasoning etc of the candidates. Proficiency test is to assess the expertise and skill of the candidate on the subject. Aptitude tests, help the employer to know the candidates performance in a manual, mental, mechanical and routine job. Personality test aims at measuring the behavioural pattern such as initiative judgment, power to convince, self confidence, temperament and complexities.

10.4.5 Placement

The above-mentioned tests are helpful in assigning a proper job to a person. Placement is concerned with the task of assigning of a right job to right person. Proper placement is necessary for increasing output.

10.4.6 Induction and Training

Induction means introducing a new worker to his job. It is aimed at familiarizing the newly recruited staff with the new surroundings, colleagues or organisation. This kind of initation is helpful for an employee in setting himself to his new job. This can be achieved by supplying the new employee all relevant information about his job and the organisation through printed/ written documents and verbal explanation by his superiors.

Training to the newcomers in the library :-

- reduces learning time for task to be performed on the job;
- improves performance on a job in which the employees is already engaged,
- develops the attitude towards their work, largely by giving them a better understanding of what and why they are doing and
- solves the operational problems in the performance of certain tasks.

Training should be regarded as a continuous process involving experience and courses, both within and without the library. This sometimes provides an opportunity to acquire an additional skill and leads to improved chances of promotion.

10.4.7 Wage and Salary Management

Wage and Salary management is very important aspect of personnel management. An organization has to formulate its wage policy in order to attract talent and to retain it for a longer duration. For developing a wage and salary programme, wage and salary surveys have to be conducted, determined and implemented and their effectiveness evaluated.

10.5 FACTORS RESPONSIBLE FOR STAFF DEVELOPMENT AND MOTIVATION

In this time of rapidly changing R&T Library and Information services, staff development and training is increasingly recognized as key tool in enabling staff to cope with changes they are facing. Motivation of library personnel through promotion, recognition and incentives plays an important role. This will create proper environment for employees to put in their best efforts. A Research and Technical library must have a sound promotion policy based on merit. The best qualified persons should be selected. Persons from within the institution should get preference in the matter of promotion over outsiders.

Following are some of the important factors which are responsible for staff development and motivation:-

(i) Job Security

Once a person is sure that his job is secured or permanent he can devote his mind, interest, efforts towards his work.

(ii) Job Satisfaction

Along with job security, job satisfaction is also must. The employees may be satisfied or dissatisfied from their job for different reasons. Employees may be satisfied with their jobs because of good pay-scales, physical working conditions, management styles, promotions etc.

(iii) Working Environment

Staff status and salary scales are two important factors which lead to employee satisfaction and better performance. Good Atmosphere can be provided by good, comfortable furniture and spacious work place to the staff. Good layout of the library and the arrangement of the furniture in reading room, circulation section, reference section etc. so as to provide inner satisfaction to the staff and attract users towards the library. Besides this there are certain conditions which have an important role to play in creating right kind of attitudes of employees towards their job. These conditions include following :-

(a) Physical Environment : Physical environment is extremely important towards creating proper attitudes towards the job and institution. Lighting, ventilation, proper furniture, equipment etc, help in this respect.

(b) Working Hours : Working hours should be suitable to an individual as far as possible.

(c) Supervision : The head of the Institute should guide and encourage the staff to bring effectiveness in library.

(d) Vacations : Vacations are also necessary.

(e) Study Leave : Provision for study leave with full salary is useful for professional development.

(iv) Appreciation and Praise

When employees of the library do their work well, the librarian must appreciate their work. When he appreciates a job that is well done, it acts as a strong motivator.

(v) Status

Every individual has a status within the organization he serves. Facilities should be provided as per the designation of the employees.

(vi) Job Rotation

Shifting of an employee from one job to another will not only increase job satisfaction for the staff but also serves to give staff a wider knowledge of the library system.

(vi) Continuing Education

Continuing education is must for the successful management of R&T libraries. Information manager must depute maximum number of staff members to participate in summer school training courses related to latest areas of library and information science. However, it also means updating their knowledge, particularly to use the IT effectively. Information managers should also attend conference and seminars on latest issues related to library science.

10.6 QUALITIES AND QUALIFICATION OF RESEARCH AND TECHNICAL LIBRARIES PERSONNEL

It has been stated that a good librarian are born not made. Librarianship involves intellectual work and a person with good academic background only can do justice to this profession. High level of professional qualifications are essential for a librarian. Well qualified and competent library personnel is a pre-requiste for any Research and Technical library. The librarian appointed should be well qualified and efficient.

Research and Technical library should posses the following qualities and qualification :-

- Adequate experience and skill, sound training in library and information science, backing of subject specialization, proper administrative ability to effectively handle money and materials, helpful attitude towards interest for work, strong intellectual, strong intelligence and retentive memory are most important qualities that a library personnel should possess for efficient and effective functioning of the library.
- Experience on the job is an important qualification. He should possess skill in library techniques with special reference to indexing, abstracting, documentation, translation, reference and referral service, reprographic service, CAS, SDI, writing of reports, carrying out of literature surveys and literature searches.
- Knowledge of various subject fields is a great asset for becoming a successful librarian. It is necessary for a librarian to have a clear understanding of the universe of knowledge, at least broadly from variety of angles, it is not that librarian should have

encyclopaedic knowledge but he must be familiar with various subjects so that he may be in a position to face the challenges of the growing universe of knowledge.

- He/She should not be bookish, but scholarly, not superficial, but informed.
- He/She should have thorough knowledge of the library collections and should keep himself well informed regarding latest information.
- Apart from having a good educational background and good professional degree, his qualifications must match the need of organization with which the library is concerned. He/She must possess subject knowledge especially of scientific and technical terms concerning with the field of specialization of the parent organization.

And above all, Research and Technical library personnel should be courteous, helpful, always willing to help users, intelligent, self confident and expert in his work. He must posses qualities of easy, friendliness and should possess a sense of fellowship, good judgment, self-control, accuracy and orderliness.

10.7 DUTIES AND RESPONSIBILITIES OF RESEARCH AND TECHNICAL LIBRARY PERSONNEL.

Research and Technical Librarian is responsible for day to day administration of various divisions of research and technical library. He has to plan, organize and direct all the main functions of the service. He must keep in mind the policies of the organization and fulfill its information requirements effectively.

The duties of R&T librarian includes the following :-

1. The finalization of selection of books, periodicals and other publication.

2. Finalization of subscription list of periodicals.
3. Preparing budget.
4. Supervising classification and cataloguing of books and indexing of other materials.
5. Selecting personnel and assigning of duties to various professionals such as Assistant librarian, Technical Assistant etc.
6. Supervising readers services.
7. Supervising reference requests.
8. Reviewing and abstracting of current publications and preparing a library bulletin or other current awareness service.
9. Supervising files of special materials such as laboratory notebook, research reports and organisation archives.
10. Attending organisation meetings research conference and seminars.
11. Preparing annual reports to management outlining activities and future plans.
12. Maintaining professional relations.

Some of these duties can be performed by other staff members if they are available and qualified. Other tasks that are to be performed by other staff members are as follows:-

(i) Circulating procedures,
(ii) Filing cards, pamphlets, loose-leaf services,
(iii) Recording and filing periodicals.
(iv) Binding procedures.
(v) Processing inter-library loan.

These main responsibilities will be required in almost every library situation. These should be worked into the flexible framework uniquely designed.

CONCLUSION

The degree of success of a R&T library depends upon the competencies and abilities, proficiencies and work environment, recognition and reward system of the institution. In order to achieve a successful programme; philosophy, policies and procedures behind it must be understood and carried out rather faithfully at all levels of management. This would also need continuous evaluation of total staffing programme, so that it can be improved on the basis of experience. The success of staffing would greatly depend on the extent to which a positive and definite recruitment programme is implemented. Salary scales, staff status, promotion prospects and working conditions play an important role in creating right kinds of attitudes and environment, leading to better performance.

Thus, adequately qualified and well motivated staff having innovation bent of mind and managerial skills and abilities surely contribute to the successful functioning of a library.

11

FINANCE AND BUDGET IN RESEARCH AND TECHNICAL LIBRARIES

11.1 INTRODUCTION

Finance is considered as an essential and integral component required for running any library effectively and efficiently. Without financial support and budgetary controls the libraries may fail to live up to expected performance levels and user satisfaction. More funds are needed when a new library has to be established. In case of an established library recurring funds are required for meeting its regular requirements and maintenance. Research and Technical libraries often serve the specialists who have highly specialized needs. Thus, special materials are acquired to fulfill their specialized information needs.

Funds are needed to build a wholesome collection comprising of documents published in any media-traditional print material in the form of books and journals, neo-documents like standards and patents specifications, micro-documents which are produced by using micro-graphic and electronic technologies. For example microfilms, microfiches, audio and video-tapes and magnetic discs. Similarly creation of staff positions for quality service require funding. More than half of the budgetary provisions may relate to maintaining existing staff positions.

11.2 FINANCE

The budgeting exercise in the first place is aimed at securing finance. Libraries are living institutions and expand with times. Libraries are not viewed as establishments earning money out of their activities even though they generate some funds.

11.2.1 Sources of Finance

The main sources of finance in Research and Technical libraries are as under:-

(i) Grants from Parent Organization : Research and Technical libraries depend on their parent organizations as they provide direct input to their intended product or service goals. Their principal source of finance is therefore, the organization which sets up a library to support its activities

(ii) Project Grants : Special project grants are sometimes made available for information support to specific research projects undertaken on behalf of the government or industrial houses to find solutions to particular problems.

(iii) Endowments : An endowment is a permanent means of support. This may be done through endowment of property or cash, creating support on permanent basis.

(iv) Donations : Donations refer to gifts in cash or kind. Donation of personal collection is an indirect financial source for the R&T libraries because such collections sometimes are extremely valuable and difficult to procure through financial investments. R&T libraries do receive donations from time to time.

(v) Marketing : Resource crunch faced by R&T libraries have led them to devise strategies to market their products and services like xeroxing, translation, micro-filming, inter-library loan services, information services such as preparation of bibliographies, CAS and SDI.

(vi) Consultancy Services : Information technology does cost lot of money. The services rendered through technology are quite costly. Therefore charges may be paid by an individual that is a member of library or an outsider.

(vii) Sale of Publication : A library may have a publication programme. These publications may include bibliographies, indexing services, abstracting services, hand books, guide books, periodicals etc. If a library is an active one it can have a publication programme on large scale. Sale of waste paper that is newspaper, magazines, pamphlets etc. can be a small source of revenue.

11.3 METHODS OF FINANCIAL ESTIMATION

The following are the methods of financial estimation providing satisfactory library service in R&T libraries:-

11.3.1 Per Capita Method

In this method, a minimum amount per head of population is fixed which is considered essential for providing standard library service. This amount can also be fixed on the basis of the type of users, such as lower, middle and top level management personnel. For example there may be an organization with 20 top management, 300 middle or top management and 2,000 lower level personnel who use the library. The salary levels of the library staff in relation to other services and the average cost of publications are taken into account for determining this per capita limit. It is the safest method to calculate library finance per head of population.

11.3.2 Proportional Method

It is a very simple method. According to this method particular percentage of total expenditure of institution with which the library concerned is supposed to calculate the funds required for the library. The percentage is calculated on the basis of financial standards available for the R&T library. For example, for agricultural library 10% of the total expenditure of the institution is spent. This percentage may differ from country to country and institution to institution. For example, in a developed country like USA, more than 10% of the expenditure of the institution is reserved for the R&T library 60% is spent on staff salary and remaining 40% on collection of the library where as in case of developing countries less amount is spent on staff salary.

11.3.3 Method of Details

In the method of details, all items of expenditure are accounted at the time of preparing financial estimate of a library using standards for each item or group of items. These items, besides others, include salaries/wage, reading material-books, periodicals and newspapers, binding and repairing, heating, cooling and lighting, rents and interest, posts, telegraphs and telephones, and stationery and other contingent and miscellaneous items. This method is also not suitable because every year considerable amount of financial provision cannot be increased, however it is useful as authority may be informed regarding library expenditure, library services, collection etc.

Out of all the above methods discussed, the method of details is most dependable and authentic while the other methods are tentative and undependable. Each R&T library has to choose one of the methods keeping in view its general and special circumstances.

11.4 BUDGET

Budget is a financial plan/ statement of the estimated revenues and expenditure for a given period of time, showing the money assigned for a particular purpose. From the administrative point of view, it is an important management tool to control and coordinate the overall administration of the library as well to as provide direction of action. It is a wonderful device to keep a balance between the income and expenditure. Budget making is essential for a library because libraries are non-profit making organizations. They are the spending organizations who has to draw funds from the library authorities. Therefore there should be a proper financial estimate of the library along with the reasons so that the funds are justified to the library authority.

11.4.1 Objective of Budget Making

Following are the objectives of budget making :-

(i) Budget provides proper estimates of expenditure on library services and resources.

(ii) Budget helps to do thoughtful spending, and limiting expenditure within the income range.

(iii) It helps in the evaluation of library services.

(iv) It helps to coordinate the entire activities of the library and improves communication with other units of the library.

(v) Budget helps in improving the efficiency of library as funds allocated are required to spent during the particular period. It helps to overcome deficiencies that occurred during the preceding year.

(vi) It helps to measure programmes of a library and their effectiveness.

(vii) It provides information regarding future plan of library on allocation for any new kinds of services as mentioned in the budget document.

(viii) It provides an opportunity for periodic review and re-assessment of the changing needs of the library.

(ix) Budget helps in organizing library services cost effectively.

11.4.2 Essentials of a Good Budget

Following are the essential tips for successful budget-making :-

(i) Budget should be as flexible as far as possible regarding the expenditure on library services. A general budget file should be maintained. In it all policy decisions should be filed from time of time.

(ii) There should be no rigidity. The funds allocated for one section may be utilized for another section.

(iii) The budget document should be simple and self explanatory.

(iv) Allocation of funds for various sections should be clearly defined.

(v) Each section of the library should be asked to maintain a budget file so that from time to time they can note down their financial requirements which are to be incorporated in the budget.

(vi) All the departmental reports should be incorporated in a general budget form.

(vii) The budget estimates should be framed carefully.

Before preparing the financial estimate and budget of the library, following factors should be taken into consideration :-

(i) Type of institution and its objectives,

(ii) Total financial resources of the library,

(iii) Type of users.

(iv) Size of users community.

(v) Any future plan regarding additional services.

(vi) Total expenditure required by the library.

11.5 METHODS OF BUDGET MAKING

Various budget making techniques which can be adopted by R&T libraries are as under:-

(i) Line-item Budget/Line by Line Method,

(ii) Performance Budget.

(iii) Lump sum Budget

(iv) Programme Budget.

(v) Planning Programming Budget System (PPBS)

(vi) Zero-based Budget (ZBB)

11.5.1 Line-item Budget/Line by line Method

Line-item budget is most commonly used kind of budget. Line by line budget is based on the budget of previous year. The patterns of expenditure of previous year are studied and new changes and provisions are made to ensure more efficient financial management of library for coming year. This is the most common and simpler techniques which divides the expenditure into various categories, such as staff salaries and wages; reading materials, library supplies, equipment, binding, heating, lighting water and telephone, insurance; travel and training, miscellaneous; etc. This is prepared year by year on 'add on' basis of existing budget. So it is also called as 'incremental budget'. Suppose prices of books have gone up by 15 %, then authorities would understand the reason for an increase of 15% amount in budget allocation.

The problem of this budget is rigidity since financial allocation for recurring and non-recurring grants are defined. Non-recurring grant which is not required on annual basis, it include expenditure such as construction or re-modeling of library building, purchase of specialized equipment, computerization of library, purchase of costly library application software etc. and recurring expenditure in nature which includes regular expenditure.

One of the advantage is that it is easy to prepare as it takes into account the expenditure of past and present. It is easy to understand and justify. But one of the major disadvantage of this budget is its rigidity because the funds available under one particular head cannot be transferred to other services whatever funds are allocated at the beginning of the year under a particular kind of service are to be spent only for that kind of service. No mid-term provision for introducing new kind of service can be made. If there is any new proposal it will be implemented only in the next years budget. This budget is not practical for collection development so users information needs are not satisfied.

11.5.2 Performance Budget

It is based on the performance of activities of various sections, units and divisions of library, The presentation of statistical information is a major support factor in the formulation of the budget. The quantitative data about all activities is collected carefully over a period of time. The management techniques like cost-benefit analysis are applied to measure the performance. It is based on the statistics such as the number of users visited the library previous year, the number of reference queries answered, the number of books issued, the number of additions to the collection and the utility of additional collection and number of ILL requests satisfied.

This budget has been criticized because while collecting the data, only quantitative aspect is kept in mind, ignoring the most important aspect, that is the qualitative aspect of the service. For example - if the cost has to be calculated for acquisition of material, it involves various stages of activities starting from verification of bibliographical details of the title, placing an order, receiving the documents, verification of the received items with items on order, accessioning, pasting and stamping, cataloguing and classification; completion of book an catalogue cards, filing cards and sending books for placing on relevant shelves. For cost calculation, each of these activities has to be analyzed in terms of time taken and average cost involved in doing each activity, Therefore, careful costing and work measurement technique has to be applied to each activity in a work programme. Fixed cost of building maintenance, heating, lighting and equipment used, must also be added to the final cost of total number of work programmes. In this way, total budget can be calculated by including all the library activities. Work programmes, work units and the measurement of the work are the foundations on which the performance budget rests. This requires a lot of time and efforts for the accumulation of data. Such technique can only provide supportive data. However, this budget is more flexible. Any kind of adjustment is possible. The philosophy behind making this kind of budget is in such a way so that performance of institution may be at the rate of maximum possible efficiency but in case the library statistics are not available then budget cannot be prepared.

11.5.3 Lump Sum Budget

It is much simpler budgeting technique, as in this form of budgeting, authorities allocate, certain amount of money to the library, making the library totally responsible for spending the amount on various budget item. This provides adequate freedom to the librarian to allocate the amount under different categories of budget heads, as per the required needs. Although this technique seems to be more flexible than line item budget but estimates are approved without an evidence of use for particular budget items. Thus, for libraries adopting this form of budgeting it would be better if they work on programme basis, that is by further allocating the available funds under various library programmes.

11.5.4 Programme Budget

Programme budgeting is relatively a newer concept in budgeting which helps to establish priorities among various library programmes. This technique is concerned with activities of the organisation and not with individual budget heads. Such a budget appears to be most comprehensive to put the library on sound basis. In this technique, library activities are emphasized, and the amount is allocated to individual programme/activities/services for making an effective use of resources.

A programme budget is a set of activities, having a common objective which can be calculated and evaluated as a whole. For example, If abstracting service has to be provided, the cost of abstracting, materials needed to provide service and overhead charges etc. incurred in the provision of the service. Efficiency, cost-effectiveness and cost-benefit analysis are the techniques employed in cost estimation for each programme. Funds are allocated in such a way that all the programmes are accomplished at the least cost. In such a programme, the expenditure on staffing, material postage etc. is to be estimated and the budget is to be prepared on the basis of programmes or services programmed.

11.5.5 Planning Programming Budget System (PPBS)

Planning Programming Budgeting System is a technique, which takes into consideration the best of programme budgeting and the best of performance budgeting. Here the focus is on planning.

The important steps involved in PPBS are as under :-

(i) Identifying the objectives of the library,

(ii) Presenting alternative ways to achieve those objectives with cost-benefit ratios presented for each,

(iii) Identifying the activities that are necessary to each programme.

(iv) Evaluating the result so that corrective actions can be taken.

The success of PPBS greatly depends on the selection of appropriate criteria to be used for evaluation of each alternative against relevant objective which combines the functions of planning them to a programme and stating them finally in budgetary terms, This whole exercise enables the librarian to enumerate programme and assign costs to them to be placed before the authorities who, in turn, evaluate them from the angle of cutting or adding money to the submitted budget proposals.

11.5.6 Zero Based Budget

Zero- based budget is a technique used for the formulation of realistic budgets. In this method, previous budgets are set aside and each departmental head is required to prepare his budget on the basis of his predetermined goals, projects, programmes and activities, thereby starting the budget right from zero. Every unit, section and department is supposed to submit the budget proposal independently, Each section incharge is asked to give details of any new kind of services likely to be started, new equipment likely to be purchased and new financial provision for various programmes. The administrative head with the assistance of financial advisor prepares the budget in the order of priority keeping in view the needs and objectives of institution. This process of budget making is time consuming. It requires the division of library, moreover the request for financial support for every programme and activity is, therefore, worked out on fresh basis every year without reference to the past.

CONCLUSION

Budgeting is an essential process in R&T libraries. It is a continuous process, involving many persons at different levels. Ultimately, it is the Chief Librarian who is responsible for preparing the budget estimates, submitted to the higher authorities for their consideration and approval.

Various budgeting techniques are available for library budgeting. They range from line-item to zero-based budgeting. One must study the various forms of budgeting, learn their strengths and weakness and choose the best one, which is most appropriate for the library. For budgeting in R&T Libraries, Planning Programming Budget System (PPBS) and Zero-based budgeting (ZBB) have been regarded better than other techniques. Both these techniques are time- consuming because they need detailed analysis and planning for various library activities and services to be offered. PPBS requires careful analysis of data. It helps to establish priorities. For policy makers, it provides an analytical evaluation of existing and proposed services alongwith costing. It is an instrument to bring the desired changes in goals. In ZBB, one has to start from zero every year, involving decision-making at each stage of budgeting. It emphasizes on setting priorities in programmes and their accomplishment at minimum cost. It is a powerful tool to carry out selected programmes.

12

ORGANIZATION AND WORKING OF ACQUISITION SECTION IN R&T LIBRARIES

12.1 INTRODUCTION

One of the most important activities of a R&T library is the acquisition of library material. The incharge of the acquisition section should not only have substantial knowledge of publishing, the book market and other sources of materials, but he should be able to direct, supervise and control the division by providing suitably trained order librarians or assistants and developing procedures to meet the needs of the library. Acquisition of documents is on the basis of collection development and services to be rendered by the R&T library. R&T library does not have the traditional books but it acquires research journals, research reports, primary sources of information searching tools and relevant reference books. Text-books rarely constitute one of the major sources in R&T library.

12.2 OBJECTIVES OF ACQUISITION SECTION

The acquisition of books is a pre-requisite for a library.

This work is so important that it should be organized in such a manner that the reading material of maximum utility is acquired without any delay and at the minimum cost. This can be ensured only if a suitable section is organized and latest acquisition techniques are used. The first and the foremost essential feature of an acquisition programme is to decide the general objectives of an acquisition section of R&T library.

The following are the objectives of Acquisition Section in R&T libraries:-

(i) A library should acquire and provide all the relevant reading material to its clientele so that the basic functions of the library are fulfilled. For example, a R&T library should procure all the reading materials needed by its research scholars for their research projects besides books to fulfill research requirements.

(ii) A library should acquire all other books on the related topics. A R&T library must procure books on broaderline subjects also so that comprehensive reading material for research and study is made available.

(iii) A library should contain all the reading materials pertaining to research and technical activities of a particular country, city, place or institution or as the case may be.

12.3 FUNCTIONS OF AN ACQUISITION SECTION

The R&T librarians job is to select, acquire, process and make available books and other kind of materials to the clientele. In fact, acquisition of the reading material is one of the important functions of an Acquisition librarian to perfórm.

The following are the functions of an Acquisition librarian in addition to his general duties:-

(i) To develop procedures to meet the needs of the library.

(ii) To handle personally difficult or important correspondence or problems relating to the ordering of books, serials, periodicals, maps, pamphlets, films and other materials.

(iii) To make recommendations to the faculty concerning with book selection.

(iv) To consult with heads of other departments and divisions concerned with book orders.

(v) To have materials filmed or otherwise reproduced when they are out of print or otherwise unavailable in original.

(vi) To supervise the handling of all gifts and exchanges coming into the library.

(vii) Maintenance and use of bibliographic aids peculiar to acquisition work such as dealers catalogues, trade lists etc.

(viii) Maintenance of files and other records essential to acquisition work.

(ix) Preparation of bills for payment, book-keeping and other financial activities assigned to the department.

(x) To receipt, handle and check materials received.

(xi) Checking and passing bills for books received.

(xii) Ordering and checking of periodicals.

(xiii) Accessioning of reading materials received.

(xiv) Preparation of accession lists.

(xv) Making advance payments to agencies and publishers.

12.4 RELATIONSHIP OF ACQUISITION SECTION WITH OTHER SECTIONS

The work of the Acquisition section cannot be

effectively performed without adequate and willing co-operation of all other sections of the library. The relationship of Acquisition section with other sections is as follows:-

12.4.1 Relations with the Processing Section

Acquisition Section is very closely connected with the Processing Section because both of these depend upon each other in one way or the other. The acquisition section would like to get the help of the Processing Section in processing of books quickly so that the catalogue is kept up-to-date and also helps in duplicate checking. The processing section Incharge should keep informed the Acquisition Section Incharge about the change of classification and cataloguing policies so that the persons entrusted with the duplication checking are properly informed about the changes, thereby avoiding unnecessary duplication.

12.4.2 Relations with the Reference Section

The Reference section is a place where the readers visit very frequently and present their problems to the Reference Section Incharge. These problems may be due to the lack of particular kind of literature in the library which can easily be recommended for purchase by the Reference Section Incharge. Similarly, Reference Books which are required in the section can be recommended. The Reference Section Incharge can easily find out the tastes of the readers and he can, thus help in improving the book selection policy.

12.4.3 Relations with the Binding Section

In case books are received in unbound form from the book-sellers and/or publishers, the Acquisition Section sends the books to the binding section before these are sent to the technical section and in this way, wear and tear is avoided. If the service of the binding section is quick and efficient, the acquisition work can be facilitated to a great extent.

12.4.4 Relations with the Circulation Section:-

The circulation section and the acquisition section must maintain a very close contact with each other because it is the circulation section which is responsible for informing the acquisition section as to which books are required and how many copies of each of such books are required.

Thus, the smooth running of the Research and Technical library is dependent upon the close relations between these sections because, if the requisite materials are not received and processed promptly, the library's regular services will be hampered.

12.5 BOOK SELECTION AND ITS TOOLS:-

The library service that is designed to provide books and to bring together readers and books, must be based on intelligent book selection policy. The selection of library materials requires constant and extensive reading, a broad background of knowledge in the literature in different fields of study, familiarity with bibliographical aids of all kinds, and a high degree by judgment. Final selection of material is generally based on suggestion and specialized knowledge contributed by a number of persons. For example, in R&T libraries by executives, research workers and technicians sharing responsibility with librarians. The librarian's professional expertise and judgment are necessary for achieving a property coordinated policy balancing competiting needs and demands against the resources available.

12.5.1 Procedures for Book Selection:-

A primary necessity in determining what books to acquire for collection is to know what has been published in the subject fields to be covered; then one must judge their relative merits on the basis of such factors as author's reputations and standards of publishers. As guides to what is in print, lists of titles from any available sources such as catalogues and compilations from certain helpful book dealers can be assembled and studied. No possible source of assistance should be ignored in the process of search and selection. Advice should be sought too, from those who will use the library, particularly from members of a library committee.

12.5.2 Tools For Book Selection:-

Some examples of good, wide ranging lists of scientific and technical books are as under:-

(i) Cumulative Book Index; World List of Scientific Books in English Language. New York, H.W. Wilson, 1898, Monthly.

(ii) World list of Scientific Periodicals, 1925, London, Butter worth.

(iii) British Union Catalogue of Periodicals, 1944, London, Butter worth.

(iv) National Union Catalogue of Scientific Serials, New Delhi, NISCAIR.

(v) The National Union Catalogue, Washington, Library of Congress, 1948, Monthly.

(vi) Scientific, Medical and Technical Books, R.K.Hawkigns, Washington, National Academy of Sciences, National Research Council,1948.

(vii) ASLIB Book List, London, ASLIB, 1935, Monthly.

(viii) Union Catalogue of Social-Science Periodicals, 1971, ICSSR, New Delhi.

(ix) Indian Scientific and Technical Publications, 1960. A bibliography compiled by the National Library New Delhi, CSIR.

(x) Indian National Bibliography, 1958, Central Reference Library, Kolkata.

(xi) British National Bibliography, 1965, London, J. Whitaker and Sons.

(xii) British Books in Print, 1948, New York, R.R. Bowker.

(xiii) Indian Books in Print, 1971, Indian Bureau of Bibliographies.

(xiv) Cumulative Books in Print, 1898, H.W. Wilson, New York.

(xv) Ulrich's International Periodical Directory, 1932, R.R. Bowker, New York.

These bibliographical sources are required to have an up-to-date knowledge of books and documents recently published. The acquisition section should also require the catalogue of government publishers, publishers and distributors catalogue, book trade bibliographies etc. Publishers and distributors circulate their catalogues to make the librarians aware of the literature available with the publishers and distributors.

12.6 ORDERING PROCEDURE

The ordering procedure involves the following steps:-

(i) Inquiry System

After the selection of books the copies of the list of selected books are got typed and are circulated among important booksellers in order to know as to whether they can supply the required books. When it is known that particular books are available in ready stock with particular booksellers, these can be ordered straightaway with them. In this way, unnecessary correspondence is avoided which is otherwise necessary. It can also be ascertained in which subjects a book-seller specializes and orders for books in the specific subjects can be ;laced with him directly. This saves lot of time and energy. An 'Order Forms File' is also maintained in which every order form is filed.

(ii) Placing of Orders

The second stage of order work consists of placing orders for particular books with specific book-sellers. Order lists are prepared subject wise generally in triplicate. The original copy is sent to the book-seller, the second copy is sent for information to the Head of the Department or other person who recommended the books in question. The third copy is kept in the office file.

(iii) Receipt of Books

If the bookseller is a local one, the bills in triplicate along with the books are received in the library. If the bookseller belongs to some outstation place, the bills are received either by the librarian who sends the same to the Order Section for necessary action or these are received direct by the Incharge, order section.

(iv) Checking of Bills

The bills are checked with the order list which is lying pending in the order processing file. The books are tallied with the bills and the order list and their editions and imprints are verified. As books are published in many editions it is most essential to take this fact into consideration. The popular edition is cheaper than that of library edition. The latter is more durable for being kept in the library because the books in libraries are liable to undergo more wear and tear in one way or other due to their constant use.

(v) Collation and Tallying Work

The tallying work includes the tallying of the prices of the books. The price is generally given on the inner flap of the cover, on the title page or on its back. For others, the price is found out from publishers and bookseller's catalogues.

(vi) Accessioning Work

The books after being thus checked are tallied with the bills handed over to the Assistant who has been assigned the job of accessioning. A stock or accession register is maintained in the library in which all the books purchased/received in exchange or as gift are entered. Each book is given a consecutive serial number. This register is known as Accession Register and the serial number is called as accession number. In R&T libraries there may be separate registers for each kind of material such as books, pamphlets, serials and bound periodicals, films and film strips, micro-cards and micro-films, maps, manuscripts, photographs etc.

All these registers are allotted a consecutive number and in such a system, more than one person can do the accessioning work if necessary. The Assistant responsible for accessioning arranges the books in same order in which the books are listed in the bill and goes on entering in the Accession Register consecutively. He/She allots the accession number to the books in a consecutive order. The Assistant puts the relevant accession number on the verso of the title page of the books and on a secret page decided by each individual library. The accession number is put on the bill against the concerned item.

A special kind of stamp is put on the verso of the title page and the relevant information is given there in. The information given is useful for reference purposes. It is a duplicate record of the books. The specimen of Accession Register and Accession stamp is given as under :—

Date	Accession Number	Author	Title	Editor and Pagin-ation	Place and Publisher	Volume No.	Binding and size	Name & Address of Supplier	Price	Voucher Number & Date of Payment	Call No.	Withd-rawal Date	Other Rem-arks

Specimen of an Accession Register

Name of the Library ....
Accession Number ....
Date of Receipt..
Supplier ....
Price ....
Accession Assistants Initials..
....

Specimen of an Accession Stamp

The Accession Assistant gives a certificate on the bill that the books have been entered in the Accession Register vide such and such Accession Number along with his initials.

(vii) Bill Passing Procedure

The Bills are handed over to the Bills Assistant. The Assistant in question, after checking the totals, gives a certificate on the bill as under:-

"Certified that the net published/quoted prices have been charged and the approved rates of conversion have been charged" The Assistant puts a stamp on the bills. It contains the following information:-

Budget Head ....
Passed for (Amount)..
Auditor's Initials..
Librarian's Initials ....

The related items on the order form or the order card, if maintained, is marked with a stamp 'Received'.

CONCLUSION

A successful programme for the acquisition of documents requires knowledge of publishers and book trade. The acquisition librarian should have bibliographical knowledge for placing orders. Sending orders is a work of great responsibility. To its traditional role of supplier of books, periodical publications and other materials, many R&T libraries have automated the book ordering process where there is access to the necessary equipment, it has added new services, such as shelf preparation, distribution of e-books and e-journals, document delivery etc. With the advent of Internet, it has become possible to provide electronic resources to users directly at their desktops. The communication between librarians and vendors and the process of seeking answers to queries or sending orders has become fast. It has accelerated the process of acquisition. All these advances have helped considerably in improving services to the users of the libraries.

13

Organization and Working of Technical Section in R&T Libraries

13.1 INTRODUCTION

Technical section is most commonly known as processing section. The work of the processing section is basic to other sections of a library. This is the section which helps in the transformation of a collection of books into serviceable form. Once a book has been accessioned and bill is passed for payment, it is sent along with accession slip for processing. Before the book is sent to the shelves, it passes through various technical processes such as easing of the back, cutting open of pages, classification, cataloguing, stamping tagging, date labeling, pocket fixing, fixing ownership slip, completion work, checking of classification and cataloguing, stamping, tagging, date labeling, pocket fixing, fixing ownership slip, completion work, checking of classification and cataloguing and filing of cards.

13.2 FUNCTIONS OF TECHNICAL SECTION

The following are the functions of Technical section in R&T Libraries:-

13.2.1 Easing of the Back

Easing of back can be done by opening the book somewhere in the middle, placing it on a flat table and gently running the thumb from the top to the bottom along the inner margin, working your way through the book to the two covers, turning a few leaves at a time, and simultaneously pressing. The easing of the back should be done carefully, so as to avoid breaking the back.

13.2.2 Cutting Open of Pages

Pages are cut open with the help of a cutter wherever necessary.

13.2.3 Classification

Classification is the foundation of librarianship. It consists of sorting and grouping together books related to a broad subject category. For this purpose various classification schemes which are used in different R&T libraries are as under:-

(a) Dewey Decimal Classification (DDC),
(b) Universal Decimal Classification (UDC),
(c) Library of Congress Classification (LC)
(d) Subject Classification (SC)
(e) Expansive Classification (EC),
(f) Bibliographic Classification (BC)
(g) Colon Classification (CC)
(h) Rider's International Classification.

Among all the above classification schemes, Universal Decimal Classification scheme is the most widely used scheme in R&T libraries as it is used for classifying micro and macro-documents that is articles in periodicals, monographs and documents of all kinds.

13.2.3.1 Tools for Classification

The schedules of the classification scheme used in a particular library are the major tools of the classifier. In order to interpret the schedules of a particular scheme, other aids as given below can also be helpful for ensuring uniform class number for particular books:-

a) Code for Classifiers by W.S. Merrill,
b) Indian National Bibliography (INB)
c) British National Bibliography (BNB),
d) Library of Congress Catalog,
e) The National Union Catalog,
f) American Book Publishing Record.

The classifiers can rely safely upon the above mentioned standard tools because expert classifiers are responsible for classifying the books listed in these bibliographies and catalogues. It would be economical if class numbers are directly taken from these tools.

13.2.3.2 Classification Procedure

The books are received from the order section after accessioning. The following jobs are performed for classifying the books:-

(i) **Duplicate Checking :** In R&T libraries, duplicate checking is the job of the Order Section. The Assistant of the Order Section gives the requisite information on the book selection cards which are ultimately sent to the Processing section along with the books. As such the labour of the Classification Section is saved.

(ii) **Determining the Specific Subject :** The classifier first of all finds out the specific subject of each book by going through the following parts of the book in a successive manner:-

(a) Title, (b) Sub-title, (c) Foreword, (d) Preface, (e) Table of Contents (f) Book Jacket's flaps, (g) The Thought contents, and (h) Book Reviews.

Generally, the specific subject can be found out by reading the title of a book but in cases where the specific subject is not clear from the title because of its misleading nature, the other parts of the book as given above are gone through.

(iii) **Allotting Class Numbers :** After determing the specific subject of each book, the classification schedules and other aids are used for allotting proper class numbers. The indexes attached to the classification schedules are also used to find out class number, through complete reliance on the indexes is not advisable. The class numbers so arrived, should be tallied with the other standard catalogues, if necessity arises, especially in doubtful cases. The class numbers are given in pencil on the upper half portion of the verso of the title page. It is given in pencil because in case there is some change in the class numbers in future it may be corrected without any damage of the book, because the earlier class number can be rubbed off. This phenomenon is common because almost every classification scheme is revised periodically.

(iv) **Allotting Book Numbers :** After allotting the Class Numbers, the classifier assigns the Book Numbers. The following are the systems of allotting Book Numbers:-

(a) Cutter's Authors Table.

(b) Cutter-Sanborne Author Table.

(c) Merrill's Author Table.

(d) Author Tables of L.Stanley Jast.

(e) Biscoe Time Numbers.

(f) Ranganathan's Book Numbers System.

Generally, author marks constitute a Book Number. Cutter's Table or Cutter-Sanborne Tables are generally used to allot author marks. Suppose the Book Number for the book "An Introduction to Library Classification" by W.C.B. Sayers is to be allotted. By using the Cutter-Sanborne Table, Book Number will be S274I. By analyzing it, we find that "S" is the first letter of the surname, 274 is the number given by Cutter-Sanborne Table for representing Sayers and "I" stands for the first letter of the first word of the title of the book that is "Introduction".

But in case of Colon-Classification, Book Numbers consists of language, form, year of publication, accession part number, volume number etc. But generally year of publication is sufficient for most of the general books. For example, the book number to be allotted for a book published in 1996, will be N96. N stands for 1900 and 96 for the actual year. A decision is to be taken by R&T libraries as to which system is to be used for allotting book numbers.

(v) **Assigning Subject Heading :** Subject headings are assigned by the classifiers so that the cataloguer may prepare catalogue cards for the same. A classifier can assign subject headings because he knows the subject of the book minutely. For assigning subject headings the following tools may be used:-

(a) Library of Congress List of Subject Headings.

(b) Sear's List of Subject Headings.

(c) A.L.A. List of Subject Headings.

(d) Ranganathan's Chain Procedure.

(e) Classified Library of Congress Subject Headings, 1972.

In case of R&T libraries the of the Library of Congress List of Subject Headings which is a very comprehensive and standard one is used. On the verso of the title page, the classifier writes down in pencil the subject headings.

(vi) **Checking of Class Number :** The classification work of the junior must be checked by the Chief classifer, so that consistency is ensured. After the Chief Classifier checks class numbers etc, the relevant books are sent to the Cataloguing Department.

13.2.4 Cataloguing

Classification determines the place of a book on the shelves. Physically, book can be placed only at one place according to the subject contents of the book. But the readers seek book through various approaches such as author, title, series and other collaborators like translators, editors etc. At that time classification is not capable of fulfilling these varied approaches of the readers. So catalogues are prepared for the convenience of both the library staff and of the users, the information contained in them should be displayed according to some well-defined rules. The transferring of technical information about a book to a card according to set rules is known as the cataloguing of books. A catalogue is an arrangement of entries showing the resources available in the library. It indicates to the user whether or not the library has a particular book.

13.2.1.1 Cataloguing Tools

The cataloguing section needs various tools for effective and correct cataloguing, These tools include the cataloguing code in use and various important biographical dictionaries, dictionaries of names and dates besides the following:-

(i) Indian National Bibliography.

(ii) British National Bibliography.

(iii) Library of Congress Catalogue/National Union Catalogue.

(iv) American Book Publishing Record.

Various kinds of cataloguing codes which can be used for preparing catalogues are Anglo-American code, American Library Association Code (1949) or its revised edition called as Anglo-American Cataloguing Rules (1967) or Classified Catalogue Code.

13.2.1.2 Cataloguing Procedure:-

The following are the jobs which are involved in the Cataloguing Department:-

(i) Preparation of the Main Entry,

(ii) Preparation of Shelf List,

(iii) Preparation of Added and Reference entries,

(iv) Label pasting,

(v) Label writing and assigning location marks,

(vi) Checking of the catalogue cards by the Chief Cataloguer,

(vii) Card filing,

(viii) Maintenance of staff manual and authority file and

(ix) Preparation of list of additions.

After classifying work is complete, the cards are filed in the card catalogue. In R&T libraries, in particular, the filing of cards for all types of material is one catalogue which is most useful, as all material on a given subject will be available in one sequence. Cards of different colours are used for each type of publication. This enables one to tell at a glance the number of periodicals, reports or patents in a given subject.

Thus, efficient less complete cataloguing is essential to trace available detailed information.

13.2.1.3 Stamping

A library stamp is put on lower half of the half -title page, lower half of back of the title page, bottom of the last page of text, bottom of the last page of the volume. In addition each plate, map and other pages not included in pagination should also be stamped. The stamp should be put properly and carefully without falling on the printed matter.

13.2.1.4 Tagging/Label Pasting/Spine Label

Tag is pasted on the back of the volume, after removing the jacket, if any. It should be fixed 1" above the bottom of the spine of the book. In case the volume is not thick enough to allow space for a tag then apply it on the front cover close to the back. If the call number is written on the spine then there would be no need for sticking tag. The tag is gummed white cloth cut into round or square pieces of about 1.25" size. The specimen of spine label is given below:-

Specimen of Spine Label

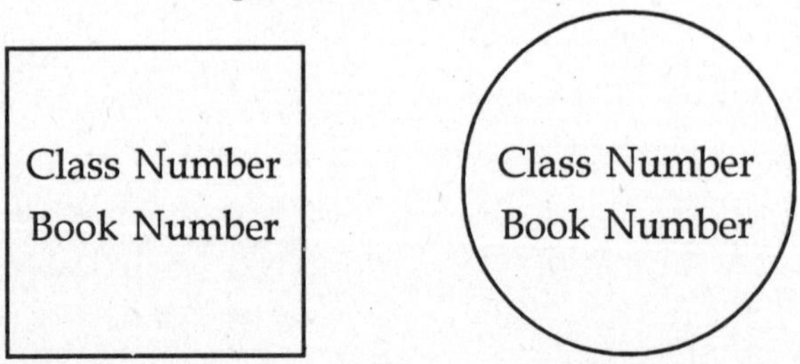

Square Piece Circular Piece.

13.2.1.5 Date Labeling

A date label or slip should be pasted on the first page after the cover or back fly-leaf of each book. But for reference books, manuscripts and other books which are not to be issued, this slip is not pasted. It should be fixed symmetrically and pasting should be done only along the top edge. The size of slip may be 5"x3". The specimen of date slip is given as under:-

Specimen of Date Slip

<table>
<tr><td colspan="3">Name of R&T Library</td></tr>
<tr><td colspan="3">Accession Number ……………………
Class Number ……………… Book Number</td></tr>
<tr><td colspan="3">This book was issued / is due on the date stamped/marked</td></tr>
<tr><td>Date of Issue</td><td>Date of Return</td><td>Initials</td></tr>
<tr><td></td><td></td><td></td></tr>
<tr><td></td><td></td><td></td></tr>
<tr><td></td><td></td><td></td></tr>
<tr><td></td><td></td><td></td></tr>
<tr><td></td><td></td><td></td></tr>
<tr><td></td><td></td><td></td></tr>
<tr><td></td><td></td><td></td></tr>
<tr><td></td><td></td><td></td></tr>
<tr><td></td><td></td><td></td></tr>
<tr><td></td><td></td><td></td></tr>
<tr><td></td><td></td><td></td></tr>
</table>

13.2.1.6 Pocket Fixing

Pocket is fixed near right hand bottom corner of the inside of the front cover of the volume. The book pocket is of 5"x3" size.

13.2.1.7 Fixing Ownership slip

Ownership slip is pasted on the inner side of the front cover at left hand top most corner. The slip may be 7.5x6.5cms, made of glazed paper. It may be printed giving name of the library. Specimen of ownership slip is as under:-

Specimen of Ownership Slip

Name of the Library

Location Place

Class Number ....

Book Number ....

Accession Number ....

13.2.1.8 Completion Work

This involves writing of call number in pencil at the back of title page and also on the secret page to be decided by the library. The call number is written in ink on tag, date label and book card to be put in book pocket. Accession number is added on the date-label, book card and written near book-pocket. Author, title, edition and year of publication are written on the book-card. Specimen of book-pocket and book-card is given as under:-

Specimen of Book Pocket

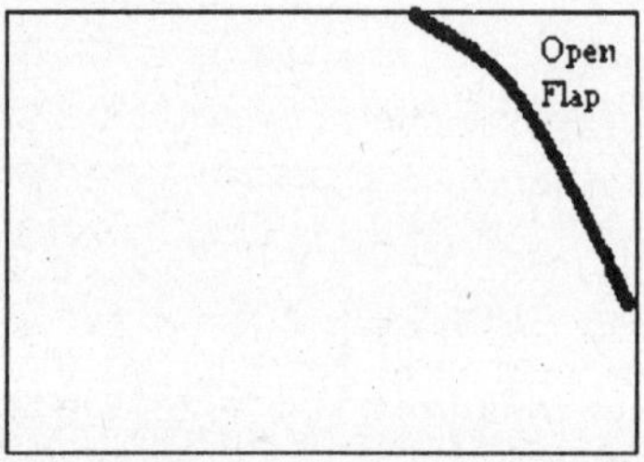

Specimen of Book Card

Accession Number ....

Class Number ....

Book Number ....

Title ....

....

....

....

Author ....

....

13.2.1.9 Checking of Classification and Cataloguing

All the call numbers and Catalogue entries are to be carefully checked by the Chief of the section. In case, no other person is available, then checking must be done by the same person. Any mistake found must be corrected.

13.2.1.10 Filing of Cards

The catalogue cards are either typed or handwritten. The catalogue cards which are kept in the books are taken out from the books and are filed in public catalogue cabinet. Shelf cards are filed in the shelf list and at this stage the books can be released for issue or put on display.

CONCLUSION

Thus, the organization and working of technical section in R&T libraries is basic to other functions of the library. Through processing, we are able to transform a collection of books into serviceable items, thus making books to be put to best use as is desirable.

14
Organization and Working of Periodical Section in R & T Libraries

14.1 INTRODUCTION

Periodicals constitute a most important part of a research and technical library's resources because they publish the immediate results of experimental research and technological developments. A continuous record of scientific advance is presented in these journals, although it is not an account easily read since related information is usually scattered among many papers. The field of research in science and technology is ever increasing and to keep pace with this ever-growing knowledge, journals serve as the best source of information equipped by the latest and correct information.

14.2 DEFINITION OF PERIODICALS

Periodicals are serial publications issued in parts as continuing titles, usually at regular intervals and for a indefinite period of time. Periodicals issue from a variety of sources. Many of them are sponsored by the prominent professional societies, others are independent enterprises while some come from government agencies. The important scientific journals have distinctive characters and maintain strong editorial policies.

According to **S.R. Ranganathan** a periodical publication consists of periodicals including indexing and abstracting periodicals and serials.

Hazel Woodward and Stella Filling defines periodical as, "a publication in any medium in successive parts bearing numerical and chronological designations and intended to be continued indefinitely. Serials include periodicals, newspapers, annuals (reports, yearbooks etc); proceedings, transactions etc of societies and numbered monographic series."

ALA Glossary of Library terms defines serial as "a publication issued in successive parts usually at regular intervals and as a rule intended to be continued indefinitely. Serials include periodicals, annuals (reports, yearbooks etc) and memories, proceedings and transactions of societies."

According to **AACR-2,** a serial is "a publication in any medium issued in successive parts bearing numberical chronological designations and intended to be continued indefinitely. Serials include periodicals, newspaper; annuals (reports, yearbooks, etc); the journals, memories, proceedings, transactions etc; of societies and numbered monograph series.

Thus, a periodical publication is that publication which is regularly published periodically and in which articles, stories, book review etc. on one or more subjects by various authors are published.

14.3 ORGANISATION OF PERIODICAL SECTION

Besides books periodicals also form, an important part of the stock in many libraries, particularly R&T libraries were there is a separate periodical section. The work which is carried out in the periodical section may be listed as under:-

(i) Selection of periodicals and serials;

(ii) Ordering of periodicals and serials;

(iii) Acquisition of current and back-date periodicals;

(iv) Receiving, recording and stamping periodicals acquired;

(v) Distributing periodicals to current reading room shelves;

(vi) Claiming missing numbers and returning imperfect numbers;

(vii) Keeping necessary records and statistics.

Periodicals section in R&T library involves the following functions:-

14.3.1 Selection of Periodicals And Serials

Serial selection needs careful examination as serials are the most important source of R&T libraries. In selection of periodicals and serials various periodicals, directories, bibliographies, review of journals were most of the journals cited are consulted. Suggestions are also received from various departments of the organisation, the researchers, specialists etc. The library authority usually the head of the organisation is finally to decide on their purchase, consider the users demand, the financial resources and the periodical resources of the library. R&T library sends a list of periodical titles already subscribed by the library to the specialists working in the institutions with which the library is concerned. Suggestions from the specialists regarding new editions are always welcomed. Specialist sometimes may also suggest the deletion of the serial title subscribed by the R&T library.

14.3.1.1 *Periodical Selection Tools*

For selection of periodicals, standard periodical selection tools are acquired regularly and are kept-up-to date so that maximum latest information can be got without much difficulty. These tools facilitate the acquisition of good periodicals. The following are some of the important periodical selection tools which should be kept in each good R&T library :-

(i) Ulrich's International Periodicals Directory.

(ii) World List of Scientific Periodicals.

(iii) Directory of Indian Scientific Periodicals.

(iv) Guides to Scientific Periodicals : an annotated bibliography.

(v) Scientific Serials.

(vi) World List of Pharmacy Periodicals.

(vii) Indian National Bibliography.

(viii) British National Bibliography.

R&T Library also circulates new serial/periodical titles available in the market through libraries circular bulletin, routine notices, book trade catalogues, reviews in journals etc.

The sponsoring organisation also publishes the serial directories with the information of new serial titles and the librarian is supposed to know the latest developments of serials due to changes in publication pattern. Serial titles are often changed due to deletion, amalgamation and splitting of some of the serials. It is the duty of R&T librarian to be aware of the latest developments of periodicals so that there may be proper selection of serials.

14.3.1.2 *Finalization of Subscription List of Periodicals*

Finalization of subscription list of periodicals is very difficult job. New periodical titles often suggested by the specialists has to be very careful while finalizing the selection list due to the rising prices of periodicals. Moreover budget may not be increased constantly due to financial limitations so the financial subscription list must be examined carefully.

14.3.2 Acquisition of Periodicals

After the selection of periodicals the next step of R&T librarian is to obtain the periodicals immediately at economical rate. The periodicals and magazines can be acquired by any one or more of the following methods :-

(i) Through subscription method,

(ii) By becoming a member of societies and learned institutions.

(iii) By Gift.

14.3.2.1 Through Subscription Method

The periodicals are generally procured either direct from the publishers or through news agents-local and foreign. Those magazines which are offered by the publishers at a reduced price, are subscribed directly with the publishers. Other magazines and newspapers are subscribed through news agents who are paid either annually or for longer period.

The subscription to periodicals is generally paid annually in advance because the publishers want to be sure as to how many copies would be consumed in a particular year.

14.3.2.2 By Becoming Members of Societies and Learned Institutions

Many national and international society and association offer different types of membership, institutional membership, part time membership, honorary membership. It is very useful for the R&T library as publications published by these societies and institutions are received at free of cost.

14.3.2.3 By Gifts

Many societies in order to popularize their ideas and programmes send free publications to certain libraries. This is common with many foreign embassies. Some publishers also supply some of their publications especially new ones so that these may be popularized.

14.3.2.4 Ordering Procedure

Placing of orders with publishers is generally both costly and troublesome except in those cases where the publishers offer periodicals at cheaper rates. But there might be delay in receiving the periodicals through agents. If all the periodicals are subscribed by the libraries direct with the publishers, it will cost more to the libraries because of postal charges that will increase as for each item a separate letter will have to be written. It is especially so in case of foreign periodical publications. It will also need more staff members to deal with this increased correspondence.

In case of dailies and weeklies, it is desirable that local vendors are appointed because if these are got from the publishers through mail these are liable to be delayed and the contents will become outdated.

Order Work : The periodicals order work in R&T libraries involves the following jobs :-

1) New Periodical Ordering.
2) Renewals ordering.
3) Backsets of periodical ordering.

As regards new periodicals it is better to procure few sample copies before placing regular orders because only worthwhile journals should be subscribed of as regards renewals if standing orders are placed, it would be better if the librarian informs the vendor well before time that such and such periodicals are to be renewed so that their issues are received in time and thus volumes are kept complete and updated.

14.4.3.2.5 Payment Procedure

Having received the bills necessary steps are taken to pass the bill for payment. According to normal procedure, a library has to make advance payment to the vendor. The work relating to payment of subscription for periodical publications should be done on weekly basis. The bills are collected and each bill is examined one by one and is verified that the correct amount has been claimed. The bills are certified that the payment may be paid to the concerned vendor. Once payment has been sanctioned, then voucher number and the date is entered in the register-card. The subscription amount is refunded if the periodical has ceased publication. If the complete volume is not supplied, then the amount may be refunded or adjusted.

14.3.2.6 Binding of Periodicals

Back files of periodicals are maintained by R&T libraries. The decision regarding the binding of periodicals depends upon the value and nature of periodicals. The binding material used for the periodicals must be attractive and durable. The choice for the colour of binding should be kept in mind. If the library has its own binding section, then the periodicals can be bound and repaired without any loss of time.

14.4 METHODS OF RECORDING THE RECEIPT OF PERIODICALS

A large number of methods are available for recording the receipt of periodical publications in a library.

The methods for recording the receipt are given below:-

(i) Register System.

(ii) Ledger System.

(iii) Two card system.

(iv) Three card system.

(v) Kardex.

14.4.1 Register System

In case a library does not receive a dozen or two periodicals, then register system may be adopted. The periodicals received are recorded in one page in alphabetical order according to frequency of publication. In this system, the monthlies, quarterlies and half-yearlies may be recorded on one page. The page for monthlies, quarterlies and half-yearlies may contain the following information.

The heading will consists of the name of the library and its location. The next line will be for the year. Then the page will be divided into vertical and horizontal columns. The vertical columns will record the titles of the periodicals and the horizontal columns will be divided into the following segments as shown in the specimen :-

Specimen

Name of the Library ....

Place ....

For the Year ....

Serial Number	*Title*	*Volume & Year*	*Publisher*	*Supplier/ vendor*	*Period Jan. Feb. Dec.*	*Subscription Bill No & Date*	*Vouncher No. & Date*	*Remarks.*

As soon as a periodical is received by the library, the date of its receipt is entered in the month column against the periodical and similar date is put on the title cover of the periodicals. An ownership stamp is also put on the title cover.

For dailies and weeklies the specimen page of a periodicals register will be as follows :-

Specimen

Name of the Library : ....

Place : ....

Title : ....

Publisher : ....

Supplier : ....

Volume & Year : ....

Subscription : ....

Bill No. & Date : ....

S.No.	Month	Days															Remarks
1	January	1	2	3	4	5	6	7	8	9	10	11	12	13	14	... 31	
2	February																
3	March																
4	April																
5	May																
6	June																
7	July																
8	August																
9	September																
10	October																
11	November																
12	December																

14.4.2 Ledger System

In case of large research and technical libraries periodicals received in the library may be entered in a permanent ledger in an alphabetical or numerical manner, devoting, one page at least to each periodical. In case the numerical manner is adopted an index of the periodicals subscribed must be placed at the beginning of the ledger. The Specimen page of such a ledger may be as follows:-

Specimen

Name of the Library : ....

Location of the Library ....

Title : ....

Frequency of Publication : ....

Publisher : ....

Supplier : ....

Address : ....

Subscription Amount : ....

Year Vol. & No.	Jan	Feb	Mar	April	May	June	July	Aug	Sept	Oct	Nov	Dec	Remarks

14.4.3. Kardex

The Remington Rand of India has marketed 'Kardex'. This is an apparatus for maintaining visible records of periodical publications and other records. It is made of steel. The cabinet is approximately 10½"(breadth)×24" (deep) × 20½" (high). Each unit consists of 7 trays, holding 504 card holders, possessing sliding dust cover and locking device.

For each periodical publication, there are two cards, namely bottom card and top card.

Bottom card contains following information

Name of the library, frequency (strike off those items not applicable), year, volume, and issue number, title page, index, reminder, volumes, per year, location, nature of binding, volume number in bindery, library has (enumerate volumes possessed), library lacks (enumerate issues/ volumes missing), title, months from January to December (date columns are provided opposite to title, a coloured plastic tab is put to indicate due date) The card is fixed in the punched holes of the card holder and plastic tab is put at the month, when next issue is due. Tab falls down or gets misplaced quite often, therefore, in actual practice, many libraries have abandoned the use of plastic tabs.

Bottom card is useful for following purposes :-

1) Holdings of the library.
2) Latest issue received in the library.
3) Gaps in the holding.
4) Location of the volumes and issues.
5) The plastic tab indicates when the reminder is due for overdue issues.
6) Record of reminders for issues not received.

Bottom card is arranged alphabetically by title. Thus these provide approach through title. This card is printed on both sides and can be used for recording information for 20 volumes. The Specimen of Bottom Card is as follows:-

Specimen of the Bottom Card

Name of the library ....

Weekly/Fortnightly/Monthly/Quarterly/Biannual

Year	No. Vol.	1	2	3	4	5	6	7	8	9	10T	.P.	I	Remi-nder

Volumes per Year ....

Nature of Binding ....

Library has ....

Location ....

Library Lacks ....

Title ....

Jan. Feb. Mar. Apr. May, June July ....

Dec...... ....

(Type along the dotted line, then fold back)

The top card is fitted opposite to the bottom card. It lies on the verso of the next card holder such that when any card holder for a given title is lifted, then both cards i.e. bottom card and top card face each other. The top card is meant for keeping record of payments made to the vendor/ subscription agent/ publisher. These cards are printed on both sides covering information of 20 volumes. The top card contains the following information :-

Specimen of the Top Card

Volume Number	Date of Pub	Date of Receipt of bill	Voucher Number	Amount of Sub	Agent	Volume Number	Date of Pub.	Date of Receipt of bill	Voucher Number	Amount of Sub	Agent	Volume Number	Date of Pub	Date of Receipt of bill	Voucher Number	Amount of Sub.	Agent

Volume number, date of publication (year (s)), date of receipt of bill, voucher number, amount of subscription along with date of payment, name of agent.

Kardex as a method for receipt of periodical publications is quite popular especially in large libraries subscribing to large number of periodicals.

14.4.4 Three Card System of Dr. S.R. Ranganthan for Registration of Periodicals in R&T Libraries

The three Card System is one of the methods for recording periodicals in the R&T libraries. In order to keep an automatic check as to whether the subscribed magazines are being received regularly so that reminders may be sent in time. Dr. S.R. Ranganathan introduced the "Three Card System" is the Madras University Library and it worked well with the minimum staff. In this method three different cards of 5"×3" size, are maintained for each periodical. The cards used is called as (1) Register Card (2) Check Card and (3) Classified Card.

14.4.4.1 Register Card

The register card is meant for recording information about the name of the periodical, subscribed, its publisher, supplier, frequency of publication, amount of subscription, voucher number, date of payment and the complete data showing the receipt and non-receipt of particular issues of a periodical/serial. It also provides information about the actual date of receipt, whether it was delayed or was received in time, whether any reminders were sent or not and so on. Register card are arranged in a tray in an alphabetical orders.

Specimen of Register Card

Title ....

Publisher ....

Vendor ....

PAYMENT		
Volume or Year	Annual Subscription	Voucher No. & Date

Class Number	Periodicity	Order	Number & Date
....	....	....	....

Note ....

Vol. & No.	Date of Publication	Date of Receipt	Vol & No.	Date of Publication	Date of Receipt.

14.4.4.2 *The Check Card*

The Check Card is considered to be the most important component. The check card helps to check automatically the receipt or non-receipt of a particular periodical issue. These cards are then arranged in a tray alphabetically behind guide cards. It makes the system automatic and reminders are sent without any loss of time and energy. This automatic check is made possible by the mechanism of dividing a year into 60 weeks and providing 60 guide cards by making them as follows :-

(60 week guides – there can be maximum 5 weeks in a month 12×5 = 60)

1.1.	1.2.	1.3.	1.4	1.5	for	January
2.1.	2.2.	2.3.	2.4.	2.5.	for	February
6.1	6.2	6.3	6.4	6.5	for	June
10.1	10.2	10.3	10.4	10.5	for	October
12.1	12.2	12.3	12.4	12.5	for	December

Check cards of the periodicals due in a particular

week are shifted behind the concerned guide card which is automatically checked in that week so that it is easy to find out which periodicals are due in which week or month.

The Process for check card begins as and when a new issue of a particular periodical is received in the library, its check card is located from behind the appropriate week guide corresponding to its next issue. For example, the current issue of a periodical arrives as expected in the 2nd week of October. Its check card will be found in the set of cards behind the week guide number as 10.2 (Oct is the 10th month and 2 is 2nd week.) After entering the details this card will be taken behind the week guide corresponding to its next issue. For example if some periodical is bimonthly and hence its next issue is normally expected to receive in the second week of December (After exactly two months). The number of the week guide behind which the check card is to be refilled is 10.2. At the end of every current week the check card remaining behind the corresponding week guide will be of those periodicals that have become overdue. The library can send reminders for them and do the necessary follow up work. This is the great advantage of the check card. The specimen of check card is as given on next page.

14.4.4.3 Classified Card

The Classified Cards provide an additional information to a reader by making it easier to know as to which magazines on a particular subject are received in the library. It also gives details about the indexes of the same periodical. These cards are arranged in a Classified order according to the class number given to periodicals. The specimen of classified Index Card is as follows :-

Specimen of Check Card

Heading .... Period .... Grace Weeks ....

Volume of Issue	Due Week	Week of Return	Librarians Initials	Volume of Issue	Due Week	Week of Return	Librarians Initials	Volume of Issue	Due Week	Week of Return	Librarians Initials

Specimen of Classified Index Card

Class Number	Annual Subscription	Per in Weeks
Title Vendor Publisher Volume Available Index, etc. Supplements etc.		

Routines Involved in Preparing the Three cards

The three cards described above are prepared for each periodical at the time of placing orders and these cards with requisite information or data recorded on them are arranged in separate sequences. On the receipt of a newly subscribed periodical the address on wrapper is checked and the issue of the periodical is kept with the new arrivals of other periodicals and these are arranged in an alphabetical order. The Register Card of the periodical is taken out of the tray and after making necessary entries on it, it is replaced at the right place. The date of publication and the date of receipt are recorded in the Register card and the "Due week" column of the Check Card concerned is filled in after withdrawing it from its previous position and is then shifted to the next week. The year is divided into 60 weeks because some months have 31 days i.e. 5th week, in which certain issues of periodicals fall due in the 5th week, and it is easy to check if the 5th week is recorded. One day such as Monday or Tuesday may be fixed in a week for checking purpose.

The numbering of the Guide Cards and shifting of the Check Cards depend upon the frequency of the periodical in question. If the publication is a weekly one, the next due will be 2.4 if the previous number was 2.3. In case of a fortnightly publication the next number will be 2.5 and in case of a monthly magazine the next due date will be 3.3.

If the periodical is quarterly then the next due date will be 5.3. (i.e. 5 denotes month and 3 denotes week). When a reminder is sent for an issue of periodical not received the issue number is mentioned in the appropriate column of the check card, which is then shifted to its next due week.

Some grace days are generally allowed before issuing reminders say one week for weeklies, a fortnight for fortnightlies, four weeks for monthlies and eight weeks for quarterlies.

Advantage of Three Cards System

Three card system is economical and saves the time of the readers and the staff. The check cards facilitate automatic reminders to be issued for unsupplied items. The alphabetical and classified sequence of the Register cards and Classified Index Cards respectively help to answer enquires regarding the periodicals concerned. It is a comprehensive accurate and self-sufficient system.

14.5 FURTHER PROCESS AFTER RECORDING PERIODICALS

14.5.1 Completion of Volume

When all the issues of a volume of a periodical are received the loose issues are collected at one place, recalling the issue out on loan. Next the work of tallying or collating of loose issues including the sequence of pagination is done with the help of the contents page (index given on 2nd page). Any defect found is investigated. In case any separate supplements have been received, then these may be treated as separate entities.

14.5.2 Display of Periodicals

In R&T libraries much emphasis is laid upon the acquisition, display and preservation of the periodical literature because the latest research developments in various subjects are reported in periodicals and consequently, necessity is felt to preserve the same for current and future use. All periodicals received by R&T libraries should be registered promptly and sent for display. These should be displayed on display shelves of periodical display rack. Preceding issues should be put into compartments provided in the rack itself so that these would become readily available for the purpose of consultation of users. Current issues should be displayed subject - wise.

14.5.3 Accessioning of Periodicals

In case the library decides to retain the volume permanently then the completed volume is accessioned. For this purpose separate accession register is maintained. The necessary details are recorded in the accession register. The volume is allocated on accession number, which is written on the back of the title page at a secret page of the completed volume. Instead of maintaining a separate accession register, the accession number may be merely recorded against the number of volume in the classified index card, which already contains relevant information.

14.5.4 Binding of Periodicals

At this stage, the accessioned volume should be for binding, publications, which are not going to be preserved are given board binding.

The binder should be provided the following instructions:-

Title:- ....

Binder's Title:- ....

Class Number:- ....

Book Number:- ....

Year:- ....

Volume Number:- ....

Size:-..........................Pages :- ....

Covering Material:- Cloth/Board/Half Leather.

Special Instructions:- ....

14.5.5 Classification and Cataloguing of Periodicals

After binding the periodical volume is treated as a book and is classified and catalogued in the usual manner. Just as in the case of a book, a shelf card is also prepared. The Classified Index Cards are arranged in a classified order.

14.5.6 Lending of Periodicals

Routing of loose issues of periodicals is an accepted practice in R&T libraries, but generally lending of loose issues of periodicals and newspapers is generally discouraged.

14.6 AUTOMATED SERIAL CONTROL SYSTEM

Computers have helped the R&T library professional staff in carrying out number of activities which are as under:-

14.6.1 Ordering involves various function

- Ordering new journals,
- Renewal/Discontinuation of orders,
- and Sending reminders.

14.6.2 Readers Services involves various functions such as

- Preparation of a list of periodicals received.
- Preparation of a list of periodicals cancelled.
- Preparation of a list holdings.
- Preparation of list of holdings with their status i.e number of periodicals available on shelf, under binding and under circulation.

For periodicals and serial control, once the data for all the titles that is the title of periodical, publisher, address of publisher, frequency of publication, subscription amount year, date of receipt, volume and number, bill number, expected date of arrivals are entered, the database is ready. Thereafter as the issues of periodicals are received, data relating to that are continuously entered.

Computers can also help in periodical subscription. Subscriptions are to be renewed every year sometimes, some of the titles are dropped and some of the new titles are added. The Master File is to be updated every time. New titles are added to the Master File. Titles to be discontinued are to be deleted from the Master file. The Master file thus updated is used to generate a list of subscriptions due for renewal with the help of a computer.

It helps the staff in maintaining records of sanctioned funds and amount expended for different categories of serials. The reminders can easily be sent to the publishers through e-mailing for claiming missing issues and thus the overall management of periodical section is improved.

14.7 PROBLEMS ENCOUNTERED IN ACQUISITION OF PERIODICALS

Periodical literature is considered to be the most important source for a researchers and scientists. No meaningful research is possible unless latest periodicals are made available to the researchers. The R&T libraries in India have to face number of problems as stated below for the smooth procurement of periodicals:-

(i) India depends very much upon foreign journals. Foreign journals arrive in libraries after three or four months of their publication, thereby making their contents out-dated especially in case of scientific periodicals. This is mainly due to defective mailing system.

(ii) Missing issues of periodicals are replaced by the publisher or agents with extra payment.

(iii) Unlike books, the annual subscription of periodicals is to be paid in advance to the Publishers of Agents in India or abroad, thereby putting the libraries at their mercy.

(iv) Rates of supply vary from agent to agent. The subscription rates fluctuate so much that even within a month of the approval of the rates of supply, the rates fluctuate so widely that the subscription agents start demanding higher rates, thereby delaying the placing of orders because the rates are to be got approved afresh. The result is that the supply of periodicals is not only very much delayed but many issues of the journals are not received at all.

(v) Indexing and abstracting journals overlap each other. In other words, there is lot of avoidable duplication in some fields while many fields are neglected.

CONCLUSION

Periodicals constitute the most important segment of the whole of the scientific-technical literature. As such all efforts should be made to supply relevant materials promptly to any community of scientists without any loss of time so that investigative work is done. Automated serial control system has helped the library professional staff in carrying out number of activities such as ordering and maintaining records of sanctioned funds and amount expended for different categories of serials. The reminders can easily be sent to the publishers through e-mailing for claiming missing issues and thus, the overall management of periodical section is improved.

15

Organization and Working of Reference Section in R&T Libraries

15.1 INTRODUCTION

Reference Section is the hub of all activities of Research and Technical libraries. The term reference service, defined by James I. Wyer is as "that part of library administration which deals with the assistance given to the readers in their use of the resources of the library". Wyer further stated that "it is a direct or sympathetic and informed personal aid in interpreting library collection for study and research.

Margaret Hutchins defined that "reference service includes the direct, personal aid within a library to persons in search of information for whatever purpose and also various library activities especially aimed at making information as easily available as possible. **Samuel Rothstein** defines reference service as "the personal assistance given by the libraries to individual readers in pursuit of information According to **Louis Shores,**

"Reference is to military". **Dr. S.R. Ranganathan** defines reference service as "the process of establishing contact between a reader and his document in a personal way". He has further stated that reference service is a personal service to each reader in helping him to find the documents answering his interest at the moment pin-pointedly, exhaustively and expeditiously.

Thus, the term reference service may be classified broadly as :-

(a) assistance to readers in making them acquainted with the reference tools of the library,

(b) instruction to readers in the most effective methods of using library materials and rendering personalized service to readers by interview and queries, and preparation of bibliographies etc.

A research and technical library is the one which is specializing in a particular subject or group of subjects or a particular form of documents. It has to offer specialized services to its specialized users. Reference section is the image building section of R&T library. The image of the library regarding its service depends upon the reference service provided in the reference section .The users are engaged in research work of the institution with which the library is concerned. They work under great time pressure, so they require specialized information service. The users of R&T library are rarely given any instruction regarding the use of literature sources. Moreover lots of preparation are required by the reference staff to provide adequate and exact information to the user of R&T library.

15.2 ORGANIZATION AND WORKING OF REFERENCE SECTION IN R&T LIBRARIES

The purpose of reference work in R&T libraries is to bring together the reading materials and the readers that the latter lay their hands upon the requisite reading in an effective manner. The organization of the Reference Section of a library has evolved from the efforts of the librarian to help readers in finding books for reading and finding facts for information . In case of R&T libraries, there is a separate reference section with a number of persons on its staff. The quality of reference service greatly depends upon proper organization of a reference section . The internal organization of reference department depends upon the total space available for the reference section. The organization should be such that each staff member gets sufficient space to work, consult the required reference books, organize the records and get sufficient space to place various reference tools.

15.3 EQUIPMENT REQUIRED FOR REFERENCE SECTION

The following equipment should be made available in the reference section:-

(i) Reference desk,

(ii) Telephone for receiving the enquires and maintaining internal exchanges with other section of the library.

(iii) Vertical files for maintenance of press and clippings, pamphlets etc.

(iv) Computer terminals for online search.

(v) Cupboard for keeping records.

(vi) Reprographic machine.

(v) Few spare tables and book-racks of small size to organize exhibitions and displays on important occasions.

(vi) Audio-visual equipment.

(vii) Card cabinets to maintain the records of different inquires, record of unanswered questions and the record of those questions the information for which was located with great difficulty and after long search.

(viii) Stands for dictionaries and maps.

(ix) Separate tables for all the staff members and enough space for work.

(x) Constantly required reference sources.

15.4 REFERENCE TOOLS AND THEIR ORGANIZATION

For providing quick and standard reference service a proper reference section should be set up. Reference tools can be categorized into four parts:-

15.4.1 Fact Finding Tools

As far as fact finding tools are concerned they are organized near the reference desk. Fact finding tools contain factual information. These tools are Scientific and Technical dictionaries, encyclopaedias, directories, handbooks, manuals, gazetteers, statistical tables, bibliographies, telephone directories etc. The latest editions of these fact finding tools are organized near the reference desk while the old editions of such collection are sent to the general stock of reference collection.

15.4.2 Literature Searching Tools

Literature searching tools are very important in research and technical libraries. They are arranged in a separate sequence in the reference section so that users as well as staff may get it immediately whenever they require.

15.4.3 General Reference Tools

General reference works include encylopaedias, dictionaries, yearbooks etc, they are placed in the stack area were reference collection is organized.

15.4.4 Reports, Pamphlets, Newspaper cuttings

The reports, pamphlets, newspaper cuttings etc. are the tools internally generated by the reference section. They are usually placed near the reference desk because these tools may satisfy specific queries.

The reference collection should be arranged in a classified manner that is reference collections pertaining to Science and Technology should be separately arranged from the collection of Social-sciences and Humanities. Recent trends demand further division of reference collection into subdivisions such as physical sciences, biological sciences, education, management etc. Along with the reference collections at a particular subject area, bibliographic publications, indexing and abstracting tools and general collections are also arranged but in a separate order.

15.5 SELECTION AND ACQUISITION OF MATERIAL IN R&T LIBRARIES

In R&T libraries, a great variety of material is needed. Books are often the least important part of a R&T library collection. The books in various fields of Science soon become outdated and their research value diminishes. Periodicals and technical reports, patents, standards, proceedings, etc are the most important part of the collection in R&T library.

For acquisition of material, the R&T librarian must know the demands of various groups of users. He should know the research projects in hand and should attend policy, planning and review meetings to know the present and future programmes of the organization. He must keep himself abreast with the annual reports, research reports, and progress reports in respect of various projects of the organization. He should also be familiar with the various publications. Some collections in interrelated fields should also be built up. It is better to acquire the material direct from publisher to avoid delay. Anyhow, the documents must relate to the core interest of the organization, and all the material needed to answer the enquiries should be purchased.

15.6 REFERENCE STAFF AND ITS QUALITIES

It has been stated that good reference librarians are born and not made. The image of the R&T library greatly depends upon the quality of reference service. For this purpose competent and qualified reference staff is extremely important.

Reference staff in R&T library must possess some basic qualifications matching the area of the interest of the institution with which the library is concerned. The reference librarian appointed should be well qualified and efficient. He should possess the following qualities:-

(i) He/She should be a scholar possessing encyclopaedic mind, retentive memory, judgement and quick decision making.

(ii) He/She should not only be an expert in human relation work but should have good manners and sympathetic approach to his readers.

(iii) He/She must be able to search for the answers quickly and efficiently. He must have the knowledge of classification and cataloguing for easy location of material.

(iv) He/She should not be bookish, but scholarly, not superficial, but informed.

(v) He / she should be courageous and self -confident .

(vi) He/ she should have thorough knowledge of the collections of library especially the reference sources pertaining to research and technical libraries.

(vii) He/She must be in the habit of reading latest literature of the subject for which services are to be organized.

(viii) He/She should be able to translate various languages.

Apart from having a good educational background and good professional degree, he should be able to adapt himself to new techniques. The reference librarian must supervise the reference staff for organizing proper reference service. The experience makes a reference librarian perfect. A good memory and an encyclopaedic mind plays a vital role in making reference service a success. The experience grows with time and with the result reference service is rendered efficiently. Reference staff are assigned the duties of preparation of bibliographies, abstracts, indexes, management of ILL, translation facility, book display, exhibition etc. Thus, organisation of reference staff involves acquisition of proper reference collection and appointment of well qualified reference staff with sufficient subject specialization.

15.7 SERVICES OF REFERENCE SECTION IN RESEARCH AND TECHNICAL LIBRARIES

In order to make reference service successful, various types of information services have to be introduced in the reference section of Research and Technical libraries :-

15.7.1 Information Services

A good number of reference and information enquiries are received by R&T libraries from time to time. The range of these enquires is also usually very large, from generic to specific. There may be fact-finding questions the answers to which are normally available in ready reference sources. Normally a large majority of reference and information questions received at the reference desk can be answered through ready reference tools such as dictionaries, encyclopaedias, directories, handbooks and manuals, atlases and gazetteers, indexes and bibliographies etc. The main function of R&T library is to make information available. In the R&T libraries which have been particularly established for the research and development wings of various industrial and technical organizations, the information at the right time is of vital importance. It could advance the economic growth, thereby enhancing the economic resources, could result in better production and greater output. Lack of vital piece of information can result in various delays in the completion of the projects in hands, resulting in financial loss of the organisation.

15.7.2 Bibliographical and Documentation Services

While organizing reference and information services in a modern R&T library, the provision of bibliographical and documentation services should also be made. Documentation services may include the following :-

(i) Monthly list of Additions.

(ii) Documentation List of Contents.

(iii) Various reading lists, documentation list, subject bibliographies etc. on the topics of seminars, conferences, research projects etc.

15.7.3 Document Delivery Service

DDS is another important service which is gaining popularity in view of the rising document prices and budgetary constraints on the libraries, rendering them unable to purchase more and new documents and because of the awareness of the value of the library resources among the users. Hence, it is a basic service for any library to supply the needed documents. In case, the required documents are not available in the host library collection, the same may be borrowed on inter-library loan from other libraries in the neighbourhood and supplied to the users at the earliest.

The British Library Lending Division (U.K), National Lending Library for Science and Technology (U.K), National Library of Medicine (USA) and others are already providing excellent service of this type.

15.7.4 User Education

There is the necessity of organizing user education through the reference section. The basic objective of user education is to infuse information seeking habits among the users, so that they can search the information sources independently without the help of reference librarian.

15.7.5 Reprographic Service

Reprographic facilities fulfills following basic information service purpose :-

- Preserving reading material issued on poor quality paper;
- Providing reading material issued on poor quality paper;
- Increasing the accessibility of documents which are unique or a few in number;
- Reducing storage problem;
- Providing a means of publication for specialist material uneconomic to publish commercially.
- The contents of the newly received periodicals may be duplicated and sent to the readers for their information.

15.7.6 Current Awareness Service (CAS)

It is the duty of reference librarian to make the members of its organisation aware of latest information relating to their field of work. Such services can be introduced in the following ways :-

- Routing of periodicals.
- Reproduction of table of contents.
- Abstracting or indexing of documents.
- Circulation of Accession lists of newly acquired documents.

– Library bulletin containing all types of useful information.

15.7.7 Selective Dissemination of Information (SDI)

To keep users abreast of latest information, many R&T libraries, use computerized methods for disseminating the selective information for the users to keep them well informed.

15.7.8 Computerized Reference Sources

Internet is an excellent medium for accessing and using reference sources. In a short period of time, it has become quite popular as a source of information. One can get information about an event, within few minutes.

Online reference sites or resources play a very important role in providing reference and information service to the users. The following categories of online sites are available on the Internet.

- **Popular Reference Books :-**

  Britannica Online (available at www.britannica.com)

- **Specialist Websites:-**

  National Aeronautics and Space Agency (available at http://www.nasa.gov).

- **Portals :-**

  RDN: The Resource Discovery Network.

  SOSIG : Social Science Information Gateway

  (available at *http://www.* sosig. ac.uk.)

- **Search Engines :-**

  Altavista (available at *http://www.altavista.* digital.com).

  Google (available at http:// www. google. com.)

  The librarian's index to the Internet.

  (available at *http://www.lii.org*).

Comprehensive index of Internet sites. (available at Refdesk. com)

15.8 HOW TO STUDY REFERENCE WORKS

In order to study reference works the following points should be kept in mind :-

(i) First of all examine a reference publication, study the title page, carefully to find out the scope of the work as indicated in the title, the author's name, the author's background (qualifications, positions held, titles of earlier works), the publisher and the date of publication.

(ii) Read the preface or introduction for further information about the scope of the work, special features, limitations if any, and comparison with other publications on the subject.

(iii) Examine the publication by its arrangement, the types of entries, information on the use of cross references, any supplementary lists, indexes and the quality and kind of articles, noting whether they are popular or scientific, signed or unsigned and whether bibliographical reference are included.

(iv) Finally compare the publication with earlier editions and check whether this edition supersedes earlier editions or should be used in conjunction with earlier editions.

15.9 DIFFERENT TYPES OF REFERENCE QUERIES ANTICIPATED FROM USERS OF R&T LIBRARY

Reference queries may be classified according to the nature of the information requested. Generally queries are divided into four, general categories, namely, directional, fact or ready reference, specific search and long range search.

15.9.1 Directional Type of Questions

In directional type of question, a user only needs to be directed. He may ask, where is the periodical section? Where is the acquisition section? Where are newspapers? Where are dictionaries? Where are encyclopaedias? Where are general - books etc?

15.9.2 Factual or Ready Reference Type of Questions

In fact type of questions, the answer can be found readily. The reference librarian would be able to find the answers from reference books placed on the reference desk. It may take only few seconds to locate a formula, a publication date, address, a physical constant etc. example

(a) Melting point of copper?

(b) Density of Gold?

(c) Formula of Sulphuric Acid?

(d) Name of Scientist who invented television?

(e) Name of National Laboratories in India?

15.9.3 Specific Type of Questions

In questions requiring specific search, one may be required to find limited amount of information on the topic, involving search into number of sources of information. The queries may be as :-

(a) Short description of radar.

(b) Importance of Vitamin -D

(c) Properties of heavy water.

(d) Propagation of Rose Plant.

(e) Background information on the following :-

Television, Yoga, Space Science, Recent Development in physics, child psychology, computers, natural waste management, archeoastronomy, bioengineering, integrated pest management etc.

15.9.4 Long Range Type of Questions

The long range search query would be the one, which cannot be answered from one or two sources. It would require the use of many specialized sources of information. One may have to consult periodical articles, manuscripts, pamphlets, unpublished documents, books etc.

For example :-

(a) Current developments in the manufacturing of aeroplanes.

(b) Information gathering habits of chemists.

(c) History of law, Political Science and Economics.

(d) All religions of the world and various religious movements.

(e) Topographical account of Kashmir Valley.

Given below are some of the reference queries and types of reference sources :-

	Types of Questions	Corresponding Examples of Queries	Types of Reference Sources
1.	Current Awareness	Where can I find all latest papers published in Chemistry.	Indexing and Abstracting Periodicals on the subject eg- Chemical Abstract.
2.	Language	How can I find the meaning of word Anthropology and origin of word Biochemistry.	Dictionary Eg.- Webster's Dictionary of English Language
3.	Trend	What developments took place in computer industry during last year?	Year-book eg- The Europa World Year Book.
4.	Books	Where can I find a list of all books on the subject of 'Information Technology'?	Bibliography or Trade Catalogues. Eg- BNB, INB.

	Types of Questions	Corresponding Examples of Queries	Types of Reference Sources
5.	**Background**	How can I find brief information on space science, child psychology?	Encylopaedia eg- Mc-Graw Hill Encyclopaedia of Science and Technology.
6	**Institutional Organisations**	Please give me the names and address of Engineering colleges in India.	Directory or Handbooks. Eg. University Handbook India.
7	**Biography**	Biography of C.V. Raman.	Biography eg- India's who's who.

CONCLUSION

Reference section is the image building section of R&T library and is considered as an important component part of the entire organisation of the library. Reference library service demands special skill. Unless a reasonable standard of qualified staff is maintained, efficient reference service cannot be ensured. For this purpose the possession of the right reference collection in certain specialized fields constitutes one of the important segment of the whole scientific-technical literature and the knowledge of how to use them are two essential things to the reference section of R&T libraries.

GLOSSARY OF SELECTED TERMS

Defined in this glossary are selected basic terms treated in this text. Readers may wish to consult other sources also for other terms used in the library profession.

A

Abstract : A summary of the essential points of an article or literary work.

Abstracting : It is a process of creating abstract.

Abstractor : A specialist or an expert who prepares abstracts.

Abstracting Service : A bibliographic service which provides summaries of periodical articles, conference papers and chapters of edited books.

Accession List : A list of documents such as books, journals, reports, standards etc.

Accession Number : A number to each item as it is received in the library. Accession numbers may be assigned through continuous numbering.

Accession Register : The chief record of the stock added to a library. Books are numbered progressively as they are added to stock and entered in the register. It may be in book form, on cards, or on a computer database and may give a condensed description of acquisition and history of each book from its reception to its withdrawal.

Accession Stamp : A rubber stamp which is impressed on the back of a title page, when the information is written in the appropriate panels of which the stamp is comprised, it gives much information concerning the records, and processing of the individual book.

Acquisition : The processes of obtaining books and other documents for a library, documentation centre or an archive.

Acquisition Section : This section of a library is concerned with the ordering of books and possibly their cataloguing and processing also. Often other functions such as obtaining books by exchange or gift, administration of serials and binding are undertaken.

Annual Report : An official publication reviewing the activities of an organization for one year.

Annual Review : A publication which reviews the literature or current research on a topic for a year

Automation : Automatic operations. Any library task performed by machines rather than people. Replacing manual with mechanical operations or computer systems.

B

Bar Code : Bar codes are strips of magnetized material stuck on the spines of books and borrowers cards. These bar codes are unique for each book or borrower card. Bar code is the language which can be read with the help of computer through a source of light, scanner and printer.

Bar Code Scanner : An electronic device to read bar-codes. It translates the bar-code into digital signals which may be processed or stored by a computer. The device is also called as an optical character reader or light pen.

Bibliography : A list of related library materials or resources.

Bibliographical Details : Details concerning a

publication which are sufficient to identify it for the purpose of ordering. They many include the following: author, title, publisher, place of publication, edition, series note, number of volumes, parts and/or supplements and price, editor, translator or illustrator may also be necessary in the case of certain books. Sometimes it is called as trade information.

Blogs : A web page that provides frequent, continuing publication of Web links and comments on a specific topic or subject (broad or narrow in scope), often in the form of short entries arranged in reverse chronological order, the ,most recently added piece of information appearing first. An example in the field of library and information science is LIS News. com (*www.lisnews.com*)

Books : A packaged carrier of information and knowledge. A division of a literary work, which is separately published and has an independent physical existence, although its pagination may be continuous with other volumes.

Book Selection : The process of choosing books for inclusion in a library with a view to provide a balanced increase to the stock.

Book Number : The symbols, usually a combination of letters and numbers, used to distinguish among items with the same classification number in order to maintain the alphabetical order (by author, title, or other entry) of items.

Book Review : An evaluation of a book published in a periodical or newspaper.

Browse : To investigate, without design, the contents of a collection of books or documents.

Budget : A itemized list of expected income and expenditure for a specific future period. The total amount of money which is available for library purposes after the estimate of anticipated authority.

C

Carrel : A small room connected with a reference library, which is set aside for continuous research work by one reader and in which books, note-books etc, may be securely locked during the temporary absence of the reader. The word is now used to indicate any table or other space reserved for one reader which provides by means of front and side screening a more or less secluded study and writing area, whether or not facilities are provided for locking up of books.

CAS : Current Awareness Service, system of documentation/bibliographic service that provides latest/current information to the researcher at right time in a convenient form.

Current Awareness Bulletin : A specialized documentation service. A publication provided by a library to keep users up to date with information in their interest areas.

Catalogue : A list of books of a collection, or a library, or a group of libraries arranged in some definite order. It differs from a bibliography which is a list of books not confined to those in any one collection.

CD-ROM : Compact-disc Read Only Memory. A computer disc on which data is recorded and using a laser. CD-ROM discs provide very large storage for computer programs and data including audio, video and graphics. It is a non-magnetic disc of 4.75" (12cms) in diameter, on which approximately 630 megabytes data can be permanently recorded.

Charging Desk : The main counter in the library where books are issued to readers and received back.

Circulation : Borrowing and returning of library items.

Classification : A scheme for the arrangement of

books and other material in a logical sequence according to form or subject.

Class Number : One or more characters showing the class to which a book belongs in the scheme of classification in use. In a Relative Location this number also shows the place of the book on the shelves and in relation to other subjects. It translates the name of its specific subjects into the artificial language of the notation of the scheme of classification.

Clientele : User of the library and it services.

Conference Proceedings : The published papers given at a conference.

Contents Page : The page at the front of a book or serial/ periodical which lists the contents in the order in which they appear.

Collation : The process of examining a new book to check its completeness, presence of all contents, illustrations, pages, size, photographs, columns etc.

Computer : A programmable electronic machine that processes and stores information.

Cost-benefit Analysis : Analytical technique involving a monetary assessment of total costs and revenues of a project, paying particular attention to social costs and benefits which do not normally feature conventional costing exercises.

Cost-Effectiveness : Analysis of benefits of particular expenditure to establish whether the same expenditure could be used more effectively or whether the same benefits are attainable with less expenditure.

D

Data : Collection of unorganized pieces of information. It refers to individual fact, statistics or a group of facts.

Database : A collection of data stored in computer. The data is integrated and cross referenced so that different people can access it for different purpose.

Document : A generic name for all types of reading materials acquired in a library and includes graphic printed and processed items.

Documentation : Art of collecting, recording, preserving and making use of the document particularly relating to scientific reports semi-published material, statistics etc. as quickly as possible.

Documentalist : One who practices documentation. An information officer or an intelligence officer who is concerned with the collection and dissemination of knowledge, rather than the librarian who is concerned with the techniques of handling records of knowledge, making them available and possibly exploiting them. He is concerned with assembling information contained within documents together with data from other sources to form a new compilation.

Document Delivery Service (DDS) : The process of supplying the relevant documents on a specific topic to the user. DDS may also be offered online to the user terminals, rather than hardcopy or via electronic mail.

DIALOG : Online search service of Knight Rider (USA). A major US host offering over 300 databases, set up in 1972, DIALOG was for many years the front-runner in online retrieval. A number of registered trade and service marks are used in the DIALOG organization amongst them being DIALINDEX, DIALORDER, DIALOGLINK, DIALMAIL and DIALNET.

Directing : Directing is the managerial function that enables managers to get things done through persons, both individually and collectively.

Directories : Directories contain information

regarding the name, structure, functions, objectives, operational activities, addresses, officers, members etc. of various types of institutions. There are directories of persons which cover information about the name, address, status, academic qualifications, professional experience, affiliation etc. of an individual.

Dissemination of Information : The distribution or sending of information whether specifically requested or not, to members of an organization by a librarian or information officer. The means used normally include news bulletins, abstracts, individual memoranda or letters and personal interviews or telephone calls but may also include notes accompanying articles memoranda, cuttings or reports and the underlining of sentences or marking of paragraphs in same.

Dissertation/Theses : Theses or dissertations are meant to provide report on some original work in a specified field. Usually they are the result of purely academic pursuit. Valuable information appears in Phd theses and M.Phil Dissertations submitted to the universities for degrees.

DVD : Digital Versatile Disk (formerly Digital Video. Disk). A optical disc with the same physical size as a CD but with significantly greater storage capacity. DVD's can also be double-sided or dual layer.

E

E-Books : A digital version of a traditional print book designed to be read on a personal computer or an e-book reader (a software application for use on a book-sized computer used solely as a reading device).

Electronic Document Delivery : The transfer of information from publisher or library to user by electronic means such as videotext, e-mail, online network or via CD-

ROM, by passing traditional paper publishing and distribution.

E-Mail : Electronic Mail. Method of sending and receiving messages, memoranda, letters, reports etc. between individuals or organizations by use of videotext, and online networks.

Electronic Publishing/Journal : The use of electronic means of communication to make information available. Publication and dissemination avoids traditional paper formats and uses electronic databases, videotext, e-mail, electronic newsletters etc.

Encyclopaedias : Encyclopaedias are the works containing informative articles on subject in every field of knowledge. Usually arranged in an alphabetical order.

Endowments : Giving a large amount of money or property for the use and benefit of an organization.

F

Filmstrips : A strip of 16mm or 35 mm film varying in length up to fifty frames and bearing pictures, text or captions. The positive images in black and white or in colour and usually on 35mm film, are projected one at a time by means of a film projector. Some film strips are equipped with a tape or a recording that contains not only the narration but also a subsonic signal that activates a solenoid to advance the filmstrip to the next frame on being given a cue.

Finance : Funds required for day to day functioning of the institutions.

Format : A term used to describe the appearance and make-up of a book; its size, shape, paper, type, binding, illustrations etc. The layout or presentation of items in machine-readable form or in a machine printout.

G

Gazetteer : A geographical dictionary with a varying amount of descriptive, geographical, historical and statistical information.

H

Half Yearlies Periodical : A periodical which is issued at six-monthly intervals. Also called as semi-annual or bi-annual.

Hand books : A handbook is a source of knowledge. It normally emphasizes recent advances in the particular field. It brings together comprehensively and collectively latest information in a field of knowledge.

Hardware : It refers to the machine itself. Apparatus used in information retrieval, data processing, the audio-visual filed, or required for consultation of all non-book materials which are not readable by the unaided eyes. More specifically, the physical devices of which a computer consists.

House-keeping Operations : Routine and continuing library operations, such as book ordering, accessioning, cataloguing, processing and the circulation etc. of documents and other library materials. In computer operations, it is generally contrasted with information retrieval.

I

Index : A detailed alphabetical list or table of topics, names of persons, places etc., treated or mentioned in a book or series of books, pointing out their exact positions in the volume, usually by page number but often by section or entry number.

Indexer : A specialist or an expert who prepares an index.

Indexing : It is an art or technique of compiling an index.

Induction : Process of introducing and training new entrants/employees on their job, position or office.

Information : A recorded message, irrespective of physical form or content.

Information Technology : A generic term to cover the acquisition, processing, storage and dissemination of information-textual, numerical, pictorial and vocal. The term is restricted to systems dependent on a microelectronics based combination of computing and telecommunication technology.

Inter-Library Loan : A library activity which lends on loan documents required by other library users.

Internet : Largest network of computer. It is a global network. Information put on the Internet becomes instaneously available and can be accessible to millions of individuals.

J

Job-Analysis : The process of determining the skills and knowledge required for performing jobs in the organization.

Job-Description : A document that provides information regarding the tasks, duties and responsibilities of the job.

Job-Evaluation : Specifying the value of a job in relation to other jobs.

Journal : A newspaper or periodical, particularly a periodical issued by society or institution and containing news, proceedings, transactions and reports of work carried out in a particular field.

L

LAN : A data transmission system linking computers and other devices within a restricted geographical area. Full form of LAN is Local Area Network.

Library Authorities:- Person or a collective body of persons empowered by law to act on behalf of the library concerned.

Library Network : Interlinking library resources and services by means of computer and communication technologies.

Library Software : It is a body of encoded information either data or program that can be read only by a computer.

Line by Line Method:- It is a budgeting method. It is based on the budget of the previous year. New funds are allocated at the beginning of the year and cannot be transferred to any other service.

Lump Sum Budget:- It is much simpler budgeting technique, as in this form of budgeting authorities allocate, certain amount of money to the library, making the library totally responsible for spending the amount on various budget item.

M

Macro-documents : A subject of great extension, usually embodied in the form of a book, treatise or document.

Magnetic Disks : A rewritable computer storage medium consisting of a revolving platter on which digital data is encoded as tiny magnetic spots arranged in tracks.

MAN : A data transmission system linking computers and other devices within metropolitan area network.

Manual : A book of instruction on doing, making or performing something.

Manuscript : A document of any kind which is written by hand or the text of a music or literary composition in handwritten or typescript form and which in that form, has not been reproduced in multiple copies.

Memory : A unit in which both data and instructions are stored. It consists of two components-ROM and RAM. ROM that is Read Only Memory tells how to operate computers. And RAM that is Random Access memory is the temporary memory of a computer. ROM is non-erasable memory while RAM is the temporary memory of a computer.

Micro-Card : An opaque microform of size 3″×5″.

Micro-Document : It deals with communication on a specialized topic and usually short. For example-a periodical or newspaper article, news-cutting or pamphlet which embodies micro-thought.

Microfiche : Sheets of film used to store text and still pictures as small images requiring a reader for legibility. A transparent microform, usually of size 105mm×148mm having rows of reduced images.

Microfilm : Photographic film used to store text and still images greatly reduced form, intended for use with special viewer or reader. It may be negative or positive and may be 16×35 mm and of any length.

Microforms : It is photographically reduced printed form of publication like books, journals, newspapers and manuscripts. Microform requires some type of machine device to enlarge them to readable size because of their small size. They are available in four basic physical formats like micro-films, microfiche, micro-opaque and aperture cards.

Micro-opaque : A copy of the whole or part of a book or other document made by means of microphotography. The print is being done on opaque paper or card.

Modular Planning : Planning a building so that it consists of a number of modules (units) having no permanent internal walls. In this system pillars are established first then roofs are build and lastly the walls are established.

Monograph : A book on a specialized subject, such as the work of a particular artist.

Monthlies-Periodical:- A periodical which appears once in a month.

N

Network : A group of computers connected together to transmit information to each other. Two or more libraries or other organizations can exchange library resources and is known as library Resource Sharing Network.

Newspaper-paper Clipping Service : A file of current events and activities reported in newspapers, cut and stored appropriately for retrieval.

Non- Print Form : Those library materials which not come within the definition of a book, periodical or pamphlet and which require special handling. For example:- audio-visual materials, vertical file materials, microforms or computer software.

Non-Recurring Grants : Grants are given for specific purpose such as construction of a library, purchase of furniture and equipment etc.

O

OCLC : Online Computer Library Center, a non-profit making organization. Its previous name Ohio College Library Centre. The OCLC network database consists of MARC records and records created by member libraries for material not covered by the MARC files.

Organizing : It is one of the functions of management. Organizing refers to the creation of an operational structure of various divisions. The structure is on determined on the basis of analysis of work and jobs of all the different activities of the division.

Online : Using the devices and peripherals which are interacting directly and simultaneously with a computer central processing unit.

Online Search : A means whereby a searcher at a remote terminal can access and interrogate database containing bibliographical or other data.

OPAC : Online Public Access Catalogue is an automated catalogue system stored in machine readable form and accessed online by the library clientele via a VDU employing a user-friendly software.

Optical-Disc : A plastic disc that is "written" and 'read' using a laser optical device. It can store digital data as tiny pits etched in the surface.

P

Pamphlets : A pamphlet is an independent publication. It is normally a document of a few printed pages usually less than 49 pages. Pamphlets are a current sources of information and are indispensable to libraries because they may contain information not available from any other source. They are relatively less expensive than a periodical or book. Since they contain information on narrow subject-field and are presented in a unique manner, they are very useful to specialized users.

Parchment : Skin of sheep or goat which undergoes a process and treatment for writing purpose.

Patent : A patent is a document giving details of an invention by an inventor. For disclosing this information, in the state gives the inventor legal protection for a fixed period for exploitation of the invention without paying royalty. A patent document provides detailed information about a product or process

Periodical : A periodical publication is that which appears in parts or volumes at regular intervals with intention to continue its publication forever. Besides the element of periodicity and continuity, a periodical publication has a distinguishing number for each successive volume, known as its volume number. Annals of Library Science and Documentation, ILA Bulletin, IASLIC Bulletin and Journal of Library and Information Science are some important periodicals in Library Science.

Personnel : The total human resources of an organization.

Primary Sources : These documents represent new knowledge or new interpretation of old knowledge. They are the first published records of original research and developments. Primary documents, include periodicals, research/ technical reports, conference proceedings, official publications, patents, standards, trade literature, theses dissertations, diaries, memoranda, personal files etc.

Proceedings : The published record of meetings of a society or institution frequently accompanied by the papers read or submitted or by abstracts or reports.

Processing : The carrying out of the various routines such as stamping, labeling, numbering etc, before a book is ready for the shelves but it may include all the processes involved in preparing a book.

Processing Section : A combined book-ordering and cataloguing section. In some libraries, a department in which the work of preparing books for circulation, other than cataloguing and circulation is carried out.

Public Catalogue : A catalogue issued for the use of the public as distinct from one issued for use by officials.

Q

Quarterlies Periodical : A periodical published once every quarter.

Questionnaire : A set of questions presented in a specific order for eliciting answers or reactions from a respondent which can be analyzed for drawing usable information.

R

Rare Book : A book of value, which is scarce and not easily available.

Recruitment : Process of securing the required persons through a formal method.

Recurring Expenditure : Recurring expenditure is the grant generally meant for the purchase of books and periodicals, maintenance of regular services the employment of regular and permanent employee.

Reference Books : A reference book is one that is consulted or referred to for a specific piece of information. Examples of such books are encyclocpaedias, dictionaries, handbooks, manuals, bibliographical publications, directories, biographical publications, geographical tools and such others.

Reference Query : A question requiring complex information which cannot be obtained from a single source.

Reference Services : Services to library users including reader education, meeting users requests for specific information and assistance, and the management of the use and loan of library material and equipment.

Reports : Reports are an important primary source of information, particularly for a research library. Most of the reports are about research and development projects in progress or completed. They may present quick preliminary information about the work in progress or they may give complete information about the work just completed.

Reporting : It is one of the functions of management. Reporting is keeping the authorities and the concerned public informed about the organizations performance, achievements, and shortfalls at periodic intervals, which may be monthly, quarterly, half-yearly or yearly.

RFID : Full form of RFID is Radio Frequency Identification. The use of microchips to tag library material and the library card, enabling users to check out items by walking through a self-service station equipped with an antenna that emits low frequency radio-waves. When an RF tag passes through the electromagnetic zone, a reader decodes the data encoded in the tags integrated circuit, passing it to a computer that automatically links data from the physical items to the patron record that corresponds to the library card.

Resources Sharing : A sort of agreement amongst participating libraries wherein each participant is willing to spare its resources with other members and in turn it is privileged to share the resources of other participant members as and when the need arises.

Routing of Periodicals:-A regular method for circulating documents/periodicals within an organization.

S

SDI : Selective Dissemination of Information. A Specialized documentation service. SDI is an automated system of information retrieval utilizing a computer for disseminating relevant information to users.

Selection : Assembling applicants for a job through suitable methods and choosing the list from among them.

Serial : A serial is also a periodical publication but each volume embodies more or less similar information but updated, mainly related to its year or period of coverage.

Shelf-List : A record of books in a library arranged in the order in which they stand on the shelves.

Software : Either a file of data, or a program that can be run on a computer, telling the computer what to do.

Special Collection : A collection of books connected with local history, celebrities, industries etc. or on a certain subject period or gathered for some particular reason, in a library which is general in character.

Spine : The edge of a book along with the sections are secured together in binding also called back.

Staffing : Staffing refers to the type, quality and the number of persons required to perform various functions of the division.

Standard : A standard is a document formulated by agreement, authority or custom of sponsors' to define a product, material, process or procedure, quality, construction operating characteristic, performance, nomenclature and similar other facts.

Statistics : Collection of information shown in numbers. Science of collecting, classifying and analyzing information.

Stock Verification : It is the physical verification of the stock i.e. it is the process of verifying documents on the shelves and those issued on loan.

Subject Heading : A word or group of words indicating a subject, representing a single concept usually found in thesauri and used in indexes.

T

Technical Reports : A report concerning with the results of scientific investigations or a technical development test or evaluation in form of scientific papers, articles, translation probably recording the current position of scientific research and development.

Technical Section : A section of a library where the functions of book acquisition, cataloguing, classification and processing are carried out.

Technical Services : A group of activities in an institution that involves acquiring, organizing, housing, maintaining and conserving collections and automating these activities. In some places circulating collections is also considered to be a technical service.

Telecommunication : It is the transmission of information by electronic means from one point to another by wires, telegraphy, telephony, satellite, radio or television.

Telex : A telegraph service enabling its subscriber to communicate directly with one another over the public telegraph network.

Teletext : A system enabling text messages to be relayed over telephone lines.

Theses : Theses are meant to provide report on some specified field. Usually they are the result of purely academic pursuit.

Trade catalogue : The information contents of trade catalogues include details about uses, size and specifications of product, the range of the product of a firm, properties of materials, design data, test results, operating instructions etc.

Translation : The act of turning a literary composition from one language into another.

U

Union Catalogue : A catalogue of stock in the various departments of a library or of a number of libraries, indicating locations. It may be an author or a subject catalogue of all the books, or of a selection of them and may be limited by subject or type of material.

User/Reader : A person using the resources, the services and products of a library and information centers. Users are also known as patrons or clientele.

User Education : It is the education of library users through a regular library course so that user may make use of library facilities more effectively and efficiently.

User Friendly : Used to describe a software package or computer system designed to be very easy to operate, even by untrained users. A menu system, helpful prompts and simple commands would be features of such a system.

V

Vendor : A person or agency that sells the products or services.

Verso : In a book, the page on the left, the side of a leaf intended to be read second in cultures that read from left to right. i.e. backside of the title page.

Verification : Determining the existence of an author and the form of name as well as the correct title of a particular work in short, using bibliographic sources to verify (i.e, prove) the existence of an author and/or work. Alternatively, verification can refer to the process of determining whether a heading input in a record matches are in an authority file.

W

WAN : Wide Area Network. A data transmission system linking several organizations may be national or international in scope.

Websites : A location on the Internet that houses a set of linked pages or screens.

World wide Web : A collection of items on the Internet in which users can move easily from one document or site to another by means of hypertext links.

X

Xeroxing : A method of making copies by use of light and an electrostatically charged plate. Smaller and larger copies than the original one can be made, as also offset plates on a paper base.

Z

Zero-based Budgeting : A management and financial system that requires an organisation to identify priorities and justify activities from 'point zero' that is without any prior assumptions. This may lead to a re-ranking of traditional goals and examination of hidden cost abbreviated as ZBB.

SELECTED BIBLIOGRAPHY

A. Lakshmana and others. "Electronic Document Delivery Systems." New Vistas in library and Information Science. A.A.A. Raju and other (Eds). New Delhi, Vikas, 1995.

Allen Kent (Ed) "Scientific and Technical Libraries to Salvic Paleography". Encylopaedia of Library and Information Science. New York, Marcel Dekker, 1977.

Amjad Ali, Information Technology and Libraries New Delhi, Ess, Ess, 2004.

Aswal, R.S. (Ed). Information Networks in India, New Delhi, 2003

Chopra, H.S. Library Information Technology in Modern Era. Libraries and Librarians in New Millennium. New Delhi, Commonwealth, 1999.

Dhar, Meghna. "Management of Library Personnel in the University Libraries of J&K, Punjab, Haryana, Himachal-Pradesh and Chandigarh". Unpublished Ph.D. Thesis, University of Jammu, Jammu, 2005.

D. Rajyalakshmi, " Library Science Education at Crossroads in India." Trends in Library and Information Science., Surinder Singh & Sonal Singh (Eds). New Delhi, Gyan, 2000.

Dutta, D.N. Manual of Library Management. Calcutta, World Press, 1978.

Heyel, Carly (Ed). Encyclopaedia of Management. England, V and Nostrand Reinhold, 1982.

Hutchins, Margaret. Introduction to Reference Work. Chicago, American Library Association, 1944.

Khanna, J.K. Library and Society. Haryana, Research Publications, Kurukshetra University, 1987.

Krishan Kumar. Library Manual. New Delhi, Vikas, 1982.

Krishan Kumar Reference Service. New Delhi, Vikas, 1984.

Koul, H.K. Library Networks. An Indian Experience, New Delhi, Virgo, 1992.

Mittal, R.L. Library Administration Theory and Practice New Delhi, Metropolitan, 1987.

Mookerjee, S.K. and Sengupta, B. Library Organization and Library Administration. 2nd Ed.Calcutta. Worldpress, 1977.

Nair, R. Raman. Accessing Information Through Internet. New Delhi, Ess Ess, 2002.

Pal,S.S. Special Library System and Information Services. New Delhi, icon, 2004.

Pandey, S.K. Sharma. Libraries and Society. New Delhi, Ess Ess, 1987.

Prasher, R.G. "Reference and Information Services," India's University Libraries. Ludhiana, Medallion Press, 2002.

Ranganathan, S.R. Library Administration. 2nd Ed. Bombay, Asia Publishing, 1960.

Ranganathan, S.R. Reference Service. 2nd Ed. Bombay, Asia Publishing, 1961.

Reddy, P.N. "Office Organisation and Management, Personnel Management. Bombay, Himalaya, 1990.

Reitz, Joan.M Dictionary for Library and Information

Science. Indian Edition, Chennai, Multivista Global, 2004.

Sahoo, K.C. Information Management with IT Application. Ludhiana, Medallion Press, 2004.

Sardanan, J.L. (Ed) Library Vision 2010: Indian Libraries and Librarianship in Retrospective and Prospect. (Seminar Papers: 45th All India Library conference, Hissar, 23-26 Dec 1999). New Delhi, ILA, 1999.

Sarkar, P.K. Administration of Technical Libraries. New Delhi, Sterling, 1977.

Saxena, Manoj. Library Building. Jaipur, SMS, 1994.

Sharma, J.S. and Grover, D.R. Reference Service and Sources of Information. New Delhi, Ess Ess, 1987.

Shores, Louis. Basic Reference Sources. Chicago, A.L.A. 1954.

Silva, Manil. Special Libraries. London, Grafton, 1970.

Sinha, Suresh C and Dhiman, Anil K. Special Libraries Research and Technical Libraries. New Delhi Ess, Ess,2002.

S.P. Singh and Krishan Kumar. Special Libraries in the Electronic Environment. New Delhi, Bookwell, 2005.

Strauss, Lucille J. Scientific and Technical Libraries : their organization and administration. 2nd Ed. USA, John Wiley, 1972.

Taylor, Arlene G. Introduction to Cataloguing and Classification. 10th Ed. Noida, Atlantic, 2007.

Thakur, D.S. Scientific and Technical Libraries. New Delhi, Ess Ess 2006.

Tripathi, P.C. Personnel Management: theory and practice New Delhi, Sultan Chand, 1980.

Wyer, James I. Reference Work. Chicago, ALA, 1927

Useful Index

The Reference are to Pages